D1491616

CLUES TO WINNING PLAY:
Detective Work in Bridge

CLUES TO WINNING PLAY:
Detective Work in Bridge

D.L.M. Roth

VICTOR GOLLANCZ LTD LONDON
in association with Peter Crawley
1987

First published in Great Britain 1987
by Victor Gollancz Ltd,
14 Henrietta Street, London WC2E 8QJ

© D.L.M. Roth 1987

British Library Cataloguing in Publication Data
Roth, D.L.M.
  Clues to winning play: detective work in bridge.
  1. Contract bridge
  I. Title
  795.41'5   GV1282.3

  ISBN 0–575–03887–X

Photoset and printed in Great Britain by
WBC Print, Bristol

INTRODUCTION

'Never make the same mistake twice'. That was the dictum to which Garfield Sobers, one of the world's greatest cricketers attributed his rise to the top.

I was reminded of this after a catastrophic session at a congress during which I drove my partner to the verge of fury – my collection of bridge mistakes had started with a bang. I claim no credit for the gift of a good memory, but I have used it to improve my game by noting mistakes – and what should have been done. The chance of a precise deal turning up more than once is 1 in 10 raised to a huge power, but it is a rock certainty that similar situations or card combinations requiring similar handling will crop up again and again; the problem is one of recognition as well as of memory.

I have, therefore, read countless books on bridge play not just once but many times until I can recognise each deal and produce the answer with little or no thought. (Incidentally, the duplication of situations between books is staggering.) Studying books gives the ideal opportunity for making mistakes while not having to pay for them!

In this book you are invited to solve sixty play problems. With South as declarer you will defend numbers 1–18 from West. You will declare 19–42 from South and defend 43–60 from East. Some examples are ridiculously easy, others very difficult.

Imagine that you are playing in a game of good standard but remember that the opponents, as well as your partner, are fallible. The problems are given on the right-hand page with the solutions overleaf. In most books of play problems the reader is shown his own hand and dummy's, and the bidding followed by the early play are given until the 'critical stage' is reached. He is then asked to state his continuation. This method of presentation involves a small, but in my opinion, crucial departure from reality which I should like to try to rectify in this book. In *The Art of Checkmate*, a French chess book on mating positions, the authors stated that if a position were reached where a forced mate in five moves would be available and the player about to move were informed of the fact, he would undoubtedly find it in time; but let the same position occur completely unannounced it was an 80% chance that the opportunity wouldn't even occur to him. The same applies in bridge. If you were told when defending a hand that unless you defended in a particular way at trick two, your partner would be squeezed fatally in the majors at trick ten, you would probably find the solution with little trouble. However, if the same situation were to appear in practice the danger, never mind the solution, would probably never enter your head.

I do not, therefore, necessarily intend to ask for your line of play or defence at the crucial stage every time. In each deal, if full credit is to be earned and deserved, you should be able to give a complete dossier on the hand, clearly indicating the relevance of the bidding including passes, the exact cards you have played up to now, notably where I haven't specifically told you, what the problem on hand is, how you propose to cope with it and above all, why.

I hope you will not be put off by the fact that your bidding will be based on a strong 1 C, and that the system played against you will vary from time to time. This is something to which tournament players have to get accustomed. I shall explain all bidding clearly so that no necessary inference need be missed. There are a large number of different ideas about defensive signalling. You will be playing normal honour leads, fourth high from long suits and MUD (middle, up, down) from small trebletons. When signalling to partner, it pays to be flexible. The purpose of a signal is to give partner information rather than to dictate to him/her what to play or avoid playing. Ask yourself what information partner needs. In particular, the following three messages should be considered in this order of priority:

(1) high or low to encourage or discourage the suit led;

(2) if this is obvious or irrelevant, then high or low to show an even or odd number of cards held in the suit;

(3) if both the above are obvious or irrelevant, high or low to suggest a switch to a higher or lower ranking suit usually ignoring trumps or declarer's long suit at no-trumps.

Discards, in principle, will be of the McKenney style: discard from the suit you do not want led, choosing a high card if you want the higher of the alternative suits and vice-versa. It cannot be overstressed that the crucial question is 'What does partner need to know?'

By way of a gentle warm-up, perhaps you would like to take the East seat for this hand in which South will deal, E–W vulnerable, and your opponents are playing straightforward Acol:

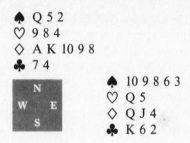

♠ Q 5 2
♡ 9 8 4
◇ A K 10 9 8
♣ 7 4

♠ 10 9 8 6 3
♡ Q 5
◇ Q J 4
♣ K 6 2

The Bidding

SOUTH	WEST	NORTH	EAST
1♣	No	1◇	No
3NT	end		

South should have at least 19 points but if he has a good long
club suit, he may have less; therein lies your hope of defeating
the contract.

Your partner leads the six of hearts which you may assume is
standard fourth high. Dummy plays the four and you play the
queen. Declarer wins with the king, crosses to the dummy with
the king of diamonds and calls for the seven of clubs; plan your
defence.

Well, which club did you play? You probably recognised a
situation in which the rule of 'second hand low' had to be
waived in favour of more important considerations. Did you,
therefore, go up with the king and clear the hearts while your
partner's ace remained intact as entry? In other words, did you
play for South to hold something like:

♠ A K 4; ♡ A K; ◇ 6 2; ♣ Q J 10 8 5 3?

You can see that if you play low, your partner's ace will have
to be played before your king even if the defence refuses the first
round altogether and the hearts cannot now be enjoyed. So, was
it second hand high for you? If it was, hard luck! He actually
held: ♠ A K; ♡ K 10; ◇ 7 6 5; ♣ A Q J 8 5 3.

'Then there is no defence!' I hear you cry. 'With the clubs coming in, they are cold for two or three overtricks.'

Are you absolutely sure about that? Before going further, have another look at the full deal and see if you can find a line of defence which gives you an excellent chance of success against a good declarer.

If the penny hasn't dropped, let's go back to the beginning. We had partner's opening heart lead to the queen and king. Declarer crossed to a high diamond and attacked clubs. I then asked how you would defend. The implication was that I wanted to know which club you played to trick three. Indeed, this is vitally important but was not my prime concern. What I really wanted to know was which card you played to trick two!

I am willing to bet that, at the table, you would have played the four without giving a second thought, but try the effect of dropping an honour! Now look at the hand again, but this time from South's point of view.

With four top tricks available in the majors, only five more are needed. Therefore, bringing in either minor will suffice, overtricks being of minimal importance except at pairs. The club finesse offers a straight 50–50 chance; note only three club tricks are needed so four or five clubs in your hand will not hurt declarer. The diamond finesse against the outstanding honour, however, is far more attractive. The odds here are about 2–1 on, about 66% in accordance with the principle of restricted choice. Note that South cannot really try to combine his chances in the two minors by cashing the ace of diamonds in case you started with Q J doubleton; he may need two entries for club finesses.

An expert declarer will, therefore, probably return to hand in order to take two finesses against your partner's 'other diamond honour' and end up two off. But that is not the full story. Even if he decides on that line, it will cost him nothing to play towards the ace of clubs in case the king appears. It is your duty to see that it does not by playing low at normal speed. So the solution I wanted was a low club from you, having played a diamond honour at trick two.

[9]

Perhaps this clarifies the point I was making regarding the presentation of problems. Suppose I had said: '. . . your partner's lead of the six of hearts goes to the four, queen and king. Declarer now leads the six of diamonds to partner's three and dummy's king: plan your defence.' You would surely have realised that something unusual or spectacular was required and very probably come up with the right answer. But did you succeed first time when I did not pin-point trick two as the critical moment?

I should like to offer a little advice on tackling the problems by introducing what I shall call 'The Magic Question'. You are, in effect, a detective saying to yourself 'What on Earth is going on here?'

Do you find that you are constantly asking yourself that question at the table, particularly when you are defending? If not, it is a good habit to get into. Once the bidding has been concluded, there are three players in action. You should continually ask yourself what the other two are trying to do or avoid doing.

Two classic examples which constantly recur are the following:

(a) You are defending a no-trump contract. A goodish-looking six card suit goes down on dummy but declarer shows no interest in playing on it. Do you ask yourself why? or do you just get on with the game?

(b) You are defending a contract and early in the play your partner wins a trick. From your point of view, his line of defence couldn't be more obvious and you cannot understand what he is thinking about. Eventually, he produces just about the last card you expected. Do you rethink the hand or just shrug your shoulders, accepting that you are sitting opposite the most desperate case in the asylum?

'I don't have to have a reason,' is a statement that has been made by many an attractive girl to a disappointed admirer. In the sphere of love, this may be acceptable. At the bridge table, particularly in top-class company, it is totally out of order. Insist on working out everything as far as you can. Believe me – it pays!

The procedure is as follows:

(i) Identify the 26 cards you cannot see.

(ii) Ask yourself where each one of them is, consider honours, shape and points.

(iii) Ask yourself what line of play/defence the other two players are trying to adopt, i.e. ask yourself the magic question, noting negative as well as positive inferences.

(iv) Formulate a plan designed to help partner and/or hinder opponents.

Please ask yourself the right questions and attempt to answer them. Most players, including many recognised experts, don't even do that. Of course, you won't get the answers right every time but at least you will have a chance. If you confine yourself to general rules, you will never reach top standard or anywhere near it, if only because there are far too many exceptions. We saw earlier that 'second hand low' was right in our practice example but for an unusual reason.

ACKNOWLEDGEMENT

I should like to convey my appreciation to Morris Leighton, whose tireless efforts and advice have ensured that the book has been spared a large number of errors.

PART 1 DEFENCE BY WEST

HAND 1
Dealer North
Love all

```
              ♠ K J 8 5
              ♡ Q 10 7 4
              ◇ Q 6 3
              ♣ K 8
  ♠ 3 2
  ♡ A K 2
  ◇ 10 8 7 5
  ♣ 10 9 6 4
```

The Bidding

WEST	NORTH	EAST	SOUTH
	No	No	1NT
No	2♣	No	2♡
No	4♡	end	

A Stayman sequence followed a 13–15 opener.

You lead the three of spades to dummy's five, partner's nine and declarer's ace. At this point, your mind should already be working overtime. South is clearly going to have to draw trumps and will probably do so by leading towards dummy. You must decide whether to win or to play low smoothly hoping partner has the jack. On the first round, you elect to play the king and continue with the two of spades. Dummy's eight is played, partner plays the seven and South's queen wins. Another low trump is coming; plan your defence.

The magic question applies here to your partner's play in the spade suit. He had the nine and seven and with the eight in dummy, the seven would have been sufficient on trick one. He can hardly have wanted to give spectacular encouragement. A doubleton was ruled out by the bidding – South will not have started with five. Telling you that partner started with four is likely to be of little help to the defence. That leaves suit preference. Partner has shown remarkable foresight in telling you how to get to his hand. You must rise with the ace of trumps and switch to a (preferably high) diamond.

The deal:

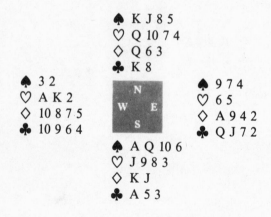

```
                    ♠ K J 8 5
                    ♡ Q 10 7 4
                    ◊ Q 6 3
                    ♣ K 8
  ♠ 3 2                              ♠ 9 7 4
  ♡ A K 2          N                ♡ 6 5
  ◊ 10 8 7 5    W     E             ◊ A 9 4 2
  ♣ 10 9 6 4       S                ♣ Q J 7 2
                    ♠ A Q 10 6
                    ♡ J 9 8 3
                    ◊ K J
                    ♣ A 5 3
```

HAND 2
Dealer East
N–S Vulnerable

♠ A Q 9
♡ 6 5
◇ 7 4 3
♣ Q 10 9 6 2

The Bidding

WEST	NORTH	EAST	SOUTH
		No	1◇
No	2♣	No	2NT
No	3NT	end	

A simple Acol sequence with the 2NT showing 15–16.

What do you lead?

From your point of view, the bidding could hardly have been more discouraging. Unless both opponents have bid very weak suits, everything in the minors is lying beautifully for them. This, therefore, is a time to reach for the rose-coloured spectacles and play for miracles. Passive defence is obviously out and you must rush to take five tricks before declarer can take nine. Your best chance is to find partner with length in spades and even if he does not have the king, he might have J x x x x with a quick side entry. You should thus start with the ace or queen of spades.

The deal:

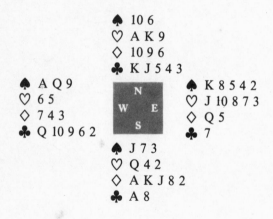

```
                      ♠ 10 6
                      ♡ A K 9
                      ◇ 10 9 6
                      ♣ K J 5 4 3
    ♠ A Q 9                          ♠ K 8 5 4 2
    ♡ 6 5           N                ♡ J 10 8 7 3
    ◇ 7 4 3      W     E             ◇ Q 5
    ♣ Q 10 9 6 2    S                ♣ 7
                      ♠ J 7 3
                      ♡ Q 4 2
                      ◇ A K J 8 2
                      ♣ A 8
```

HAND 3
Dealer South
E–W Vulnerable

♠ 9 3
♡ J 9 5 4
♢ A 10 6 3
♣ 9 7 2

The Bidding

SOUTH	WEST	NORTH	EAST
1♠	No	4♣	No
4♠	No	No	5♣
5♠	No	No	Double
end			

The opening bid showed 11–15 and at least five spades. North's
4♣ bid showed values for game at least, two aces and no
singleton or void.

What do you lead?

The magic question applies to your partner's bidding. To compete at the five-level, particularly at this vulnerability, he surely must have tremendous clubs; yet he did not double 4♣ – strange. His double of 5♣ completes the picture. While he wants to play in clubs, he does not want you to lead one. This can only be because of a red-suit void. The lead of the ace of diamonds caters for either possibility; your opponents' bidding suggests that one club trick will be available to the defence.

The deal:

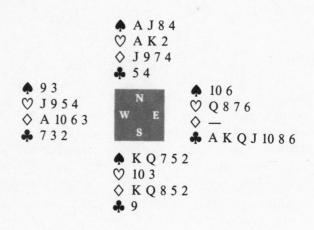

```
                    ♠ A J 8 4
                    ♡ A K 2
                    ◇ J 9 7 4
                    ♣ 5 4
  ♠ 9 3                              ♠ 10 6
  ♡ J 9 5 4            N            ♡ Q 8 7 6
  ◇ A 10 6 3       W       E        ◇ —
  ♣ 7 3 2              S            ♣ A K Q J 10 8 6
                    ♠ K Q 7 5 2
                    ♡ 10 3
                    ◇ K Q 8 5 2
                    ♣ 9
```

HAND 4
Dealer West
Game all

♠ A Q 5 3
♡ A 3 2
◇ A 10 8 6 5 2
♣ —

The Bidding

WEST	NORTH	EAST	SOUTH
1◇	Double	No	3♣
No	3◇	No	3♡
No	4♡	end	

Your opening bid showed 11–15 with at least three diamonds.
South's 3♣ showed about 8–10, non-forcing, and North's 3◇
was an unassuming cue-bid, asking for further information and
forcing, at least, to suit agreement.

What do you lead?

With 14 points in your hand and opponents in game, a roll-call on points tells you that partner cannot have much more than a jack or two. The crucial card is the king of spades. If North has it you will need to get partner in for a club ruff. If South has it, you must sit back and wait for four tricks in your own hand. To establish which line of defence is required, while keeping your trump holding intact, you must cash your ace of diamonds and look at dummy. If the king of spades appears, play the queen or lower spade, hoping partner has the jack. If not, exit passively and wait for two spade tricks.

The deal:

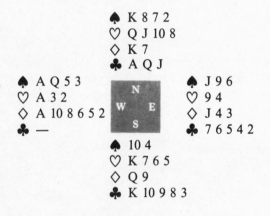

```
              ♠ K 8 7 2
              ♡ Q J 10 8
              ◇ K 7
              ♣ A Q J
  ♠ A Q 5 3        N        ♠ J 9 6
  ♡ A 3 2                   ♡ 9 4
  ◇ A 10 8 6 5 2  W   E     ◇ J 4 3
  ♣ —               S       ♣ 7 6 5 4 2
              ♠ 10 4
              ♡ K 7 6 5
              ◇ Q 9
              ♣ K 10 9 8 3
```

As the cards lie, you defeat the contract if you lead the ace of diamonds or the queen or lower spade. In the latter case, I think you must count yourself a bit lucky that North did not have the jack of spades and South the king.

HAND 5
Dealer North
N–S Vulnerable

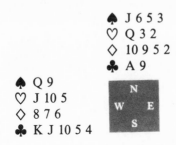

♠ J 6 5 3
♥ Q 3 2
♦ 10 9 5 2
♣ A 9

♠ Q 9
♥ J 10 5
♦ 8 7 6
♣ K J 10 5 4

The Bidding

WEST	NORTH	EAST	SOUTH
	No	No	1♣
No	1♦	No	1NT
No	2♣	No	2♠
No	3♠	No	4♠
end			

South's opening bid showed 16 plus and North's 1♦ was negative, less than 8. The 1NT rebid showed 16–19, balanced and Stayman followed.

You lead the jack of hearts to dummy's queen, partner's six and South's seven. The two of diamonds follows to partner's three, South's queen winning. Now the three of clubs; you put on the jack, which holds, partner playing the two. Your ten of hearts is won by South's ace, partner playing the four. South now cashes the ace of diamonds, all playing low, then the king of hearts and the ace of clubs in dummy, partner following with the eight. The three of spades is now led. Partner plays the two and South's king wins. Declarer now leads the four of spades; plan your defence.

Declarer has clearly tried to set up a cross-ruff but needs to draw exactly two rounds of trumps before this can materialise. You must realise that partner has the ace of trumps and must also have the ten if the defence is to have a chance. Accordingly, you should have dropped your queen under the king so that partner can insist on a third round of trumps.

The deal:

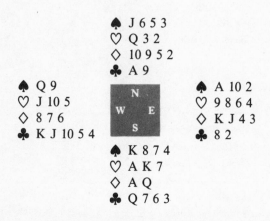

```
                    ♠ J 6 5 3
                    ♡ Q 3 2
                    ◇ 10 9 5 2
                    ♣ A 9
     ♠ Q 9                          ♠ A 10 2
     ♡ J 10 5          N            ♡ 9 8 6 4
     ◇ 8 7 6       W       E        ◇ K J 4 3
     ♣ K J 10 5 4      S            ♣ 8 2
                    ♠ K 8 7 4
                    ♡ A K 7
                    ◇ A Q
                    ♣ Q 7 6 3
```

Declarer had the right idea but his order of play was poor; the diamond finesse can wait. He should have played a round of trumps at trick two before it was clear to the defenders what was happening. In with the jack of clubs, West can cash the queen of trumps but East's ace is stranded. If South adopts this line, West can hardly be criticised for failing to unblock at this early stage.

HAND 6
Dealer East
E–W Vulnerable

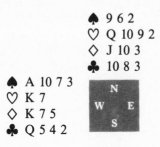

```
                    ♠ 9 6 2
                    ♡ Q 10 9 2
                    ◇ J 10 3
                    ♣ 10 8 3
        ♠ A 10 7 3        N
        ♡ K 7         W        E
        ◇ K 7 5           S
        ♣ Q 5 4 2
```

The Bidding

WEST	NORTH	EAST	SOUTH
		No	1♡
Double	2♡	3♣	3♡
end			

You lead the two of clubs to partner's king. He tries to cash the ace but declarer ruffs and leads the four of diamonds; plan your defence.

With partner having already produced A K J of clubs, he can scarcely have more than another jack otherwise with a good five-card suit, he would have competed further. You will need to assume that he has the jack of spades. Declarer has also seen the play to the first two tricks and he too knows the situation. You should have realised what declarer was up to. If you play low to this trick, dummy will win and the last club will be ruffed. The ace and queen of diamonds will follow leaving you to lead. You can safely get off play with a low spade but the ace and another trump will put you back in again and you will now be fatally endplayed.

The deal:

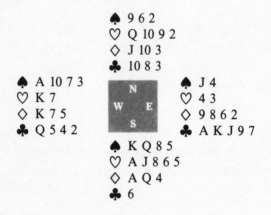

```
            ♠ 9 6 2
            ♡ Q 10 9 2
            ◇ J 10 3
            ♣ 10 8 3
♠ A 10 7 3              ♠ J 4
♡ K 7          N        ♡ 4 3
◇ K 7 5      W   E      ◇ 9 8 6 2
♣ Q 5 4 2      S        ♣ A K J 9 7
            ♠ K Q 8 5
            ♡ A J 8 6 5
            ◇ A Q 4
            ♣ 6
```

To avoid trouble, you must rise with the king of diamonds now and return a diamond, keeping your clubs as exit cards. The defence must now come to five tricks. In truth, your partner's play was far from perfect on this occasion. He ought to have used his only chance to lead to push a spade or diamond through declarer. He decided, however, that as North was so weak, a totally passive approach was in order. Even then, he could have improved on his chosen line by winning the first trick with the ace of clubs and returning a low one rather than pin-point every card for South's benefit.

HAND 7
Dealer South
Game all

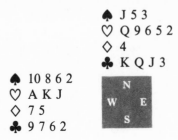

```
              ♠ J 5 3
              ♡ Q 9 6 5 2
              ◇ 4
              ♣ K Q J 3
  ♠ 10 8 6 2        N
  ♡ A K J       W       E
  ◇ 7 5             S
  ♣ 9 7 6 2
```

The Bidding

SOUTH	WEST	NORTH	EAST
1NT	No	2◇	Double
2♡	No	3♣	No
4♡	end		

After the 13–15 1NT, North transferred to hearts and partner's double showed a powerful diamond suit. Now South had the option to pass or accept the transfer immediately. Had he passed, North would have been obliged to redouble, after which South would have closed the auction with 2♡. As it went, South showed marked interest in hearts and North valued up his diamond singleton as justification to bid on.

You lead the seven of diamonds to the four, king and three. Partner returns the seven of spades to declarer's ace; plan your defence.

South's bidding almost certainly guarantees a maximum and four hearts, particularly as you know his hearts are very poor. Partner clearly has ace and king of diamonds and probably the jack as well, leaving South with the rest of the points. Your only hope therefore, is that partner's singleton heart is the ten in which case South has two equally good lines of playing trumps and may well go wrong. Your partner's bidding suggests that he might have an ace or king outside his suit rather than a singleton ten. Thus if you smoothly play the jack on the first lead, declarer is more likely to duck than go up. The other point is that you must play a discouraging two of spades on this trick. If you don't, South may realise that you are trying to fool him and may suspect that you know the trump position.

The deal:

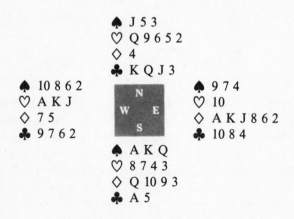

```
              ♠ J 5 3
              ♡ Q 9 6 5 2
              ◇ 4
              ♣ K Q J 3
♠ 10 8 6 2                      ♠ 9 7 4
♡ A K J            N            ♡ 10
◇ 7 5          W       E        ◇ A K J 8 6 2
♣ 9 7 6 2          S            ♣ 10 8 4
              ♠ A K Q
              ♡ 8 7 4 3
              ◇ Q 10 9 3
              ♣ A 5
```

HAND 8
Dealer West
Love all

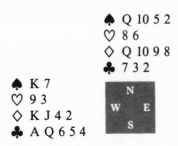

♠ Q 10 5 2
♥ 8 6
♦ Q 10 9 8
♣ 7 3 2

♠ K 7
♥ 9 3
♦ K J 4 2
♣ A Q 6 5 4

N
W   E
S

The Bidding

WEST	NORTH	EAST	SOUTH
1♦	No	No	2♦
No	2♠	No	4♥
end			

The system does not enable you to bid the club suit first. South's cue bid shows a very strong hand forcing to suit agreement and he is likely to have the values for at least an Acol two-opener.

A dreadful hand to lead from and you do well to pick the two of diamonds which fetches the eight, six and ace from South. He now leads the ace of spades; plan your defence.

South's failure to draw trumps suggests a broken holding and any finesse is going to be right. Your aim, therefore, must be to keep him off the table. Play low now; win the next round and exit with the king of diamonds. This will be ruffed and the queen will be set up, but it is of no use to declarer who must lose four tricks and the contract against this simple, passive defence.

The deal:

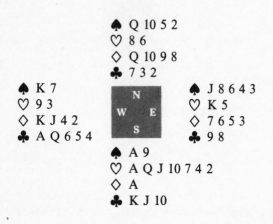

♠ Q 10 5 2
♡ 8 6
◇ Q 10 9 8
♣ 7 3 2

♠ K 7
♡ 9 3
◇ K J 4 2
♣ A Q 6 5 4

♠ J 8 6 4 3
♡ K 5
◇ 7 6 5 3
♣ 9 8

♠ A 9
♡ A Q J 10 7 4 2
◇ A
♣ K J 10

HAND 9
Dealer North
E–W Vulnerable

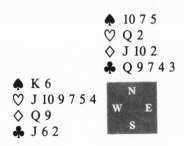

```
                            ♠ 10 7 5
                            ♡ Q 2
                            ◇ J 10 2
                            ♣ Q 9 7 4 3
        ♠ K 6             ┌─────────┐
        ♡ J 10 9 7 5 4    │    N    │
        ◇ Q 9             │  W   E  │
        ♣ J 6 2           │    S    │
                          └─────────┘
```

The Bidding

WEST	NORTH	EAST	SOUTH
	No	1◇	Double
1♡	2♣	No	No
2♡	No	No	2♠
end			

Your partner's opener showed 11–15, 3 plus diamonds.

You lead the queen of diamonds which holds, partner playing
the three. When you play the nine, partner takes his king and
cashes his ace on which you discard the five of hearts while the
others follow. Now the six of hearts from partner is won by
declarer's king and he cashes the ace, partner playing the eight.
South next leads the two of spades. You smoothly play low and
dummy's ten fetches partner's queen. He returns the three of
spades to South's jack and your king. How do you defend from
here?

You have already taken five tricks and have a complete count on the hand. The bidding indicates that the two top clubs are split. If partner has the ace, the contract must fail. If he has the king, it will be fatal to touch the suit if South has ♣ A 10 x. In that event, you can give a ruff and discard without damaging your cause. You should therefore exit with a heart.

The deal:

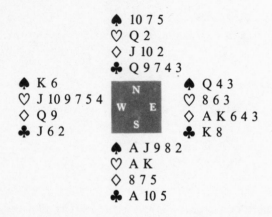

```
                    ♠ 10 7 5
                    ♡ Q 2
                    ◇ J 10 2
                    ♣ Q 9 7 4 3
     ♠ K 6              N           ♠ Q 4 3
     ♡ J 10 9 7 5 4  W     E        ♡ 8 6 3
     ◇ Q 9              S           ◇ A K 6 4 3
     ♣ J 6 2                        ♣ K 8
                    ♠ A J 9 8 2
                    ♡ A K
                    ◇ 8 7 5
                    ♣ A 10 5
```

HAND 10
Dealer East
Game all

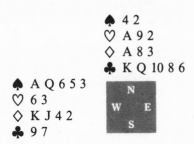

```
              ♠ 4 2
              ♡ A 9 2
              ◇ A 8 3
              ♣ K Q 10 8 6
  ♠ A Q 6 5 3
  ♡ 6 3
  ◇ K J 4 2
  ♣ 9 7
```

The Bidding

WEST	NORTH	EAST	SOUTH
		2♡	No
No	3♣	No	3♠
Double	end		

Your partner showed 7–10 with exactly six hearts to at least one honour.

You lead the six of hearts to dummy's ace, partner's eight and South's four. On the four of spades, partner discards the seven of hearts and you allow South's jack to hold. He now plays the ten of spades; plan your defence (partner's next discard is the five of hearts).

There is clearly no point in holding up spades any longer and plenty of scope for the magic question. You should have noticed three things. Firstly, the declarer went straight up with the ace of hearts when he could have cut communications by ducking. Remember, he knows the heart distribution. Secondly, partner discarded only hearts. Thirdly, he discarded them high-low. The evidence adds up to an open book. Declarer was clearly not frightened of a trump promotion. That implies that he was frightened of something else. Partner clearly has worthwhile holdings in both minor suits; and his preference is for diamonds. If you play another heart now, what will partner think? He is sure to play a third one with disastrous results.

The deal:

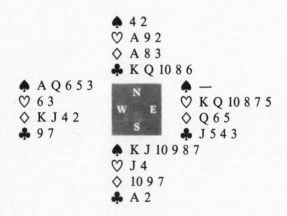

```
                    ♠ 4 2
                    ♡ A 9 2
                    ◇ A 8 3
                    ♣ K Q 10 8 6
♠ A Q 6 5 3       ┌─────────┐      ♠ —
♡ 6 3             │    N    │      ♡ K Q 10 8 7 5
◇ K J 4 2         │ W     E │      ◇ Q 6 5
♣ 9 7             │    S    │      ♣ J 5 4 3
                  └─────────┘
                    ♠ K J 10 9 8 7
                    ♡ J 4
                    ◇ 10 9 7
                    ♣ A 2
```

South will ruff and you can no longer defeat the contract. Admittedly, partner can set the hand if he, too, asks himself about the play at trick one but should he trust you or South? You should take charge by switching to a diamond at once.

HAND 11
Dealer South
Love all

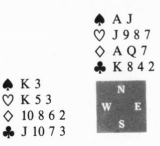

```
                    ♠ A J
                    ♡ J 9 8 7
                    ◇ A Q 7
                    ♣ K 8 4 2
        ♠ K 3
        ♡ K 5 3          N
        ◇ 10 8 6 2    W      E
        ♣ J 10 7 3       S
```

The Bidding

SOUTH	WEST	NORTH	EAST
1♠	No	2♣	No
2NT	No	3NT	end

South's bidding showed 11–13, exactly five spades and an otherwise balanced hand.

Unable to think of anything better, you lead the three of hearts. Dummy plays low and your partner's ten loses to South's ace. He continues with the six of hearts; plan your defence.

The play so far marks partner with the queen of hearts so South is going to get a second trick in the suit if he knocks out both outstanding honours. But that is a lot of hard work for one extra trick. The implication is that he has the other eight set up already. In addition to that, you see that opposite a five-card suit, dummy has produced A J and yet declarer has shown no interest. This can be for one of two reasons. Either he has the tricks set up or his spades are so poor that they offer no hope; and you know which it is. You can credit South with ace of hearts, king of diamonds, ace, queen of clubs for 13 points and eight top tricks: three in each minor and the two major aces. That leaves the queen of spades for East. If he has good intermediates, you have a chance if you rise with the king of hearts and switch to the king of spades.

The deal:

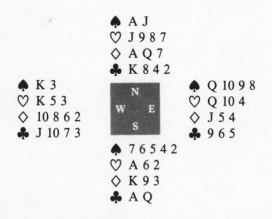

<pre>
              ♠ A J
              ♡ J 9 8 7
              ◇ A Q 7
              ♣ K 8 4 2
♠ K 3   ♠ Q 10 9 8
♡ K 5 3   N   ♡ Q 10 4
◇ 10 8 6 2   W   E   ◇ J 5 4
♣ J 10 7 3   S   ♣ 9 6 5
              ♠ 7 6 5 4 2
              ♡ A 6 2
              ◇ K 9 3
              ♣ A Q
</pre>

With partner's entry kept intact, South has no answer.

HAND 12
Dealer West
N–S Vulnerable

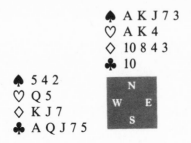

```
                    ♠ A K J 7 3
                    ♡ A K 4
                    ◇ 10 8 4 3
                    ♣ 10
    ♠ 5 4 2          ┌─────────┐
    ♡ Q 5            │    N    │
    ◇ K J 7          │ W     E │
    ♣ A Q J 7 5      │    S    │
                     └─────────┘
```

The Bidding

WEST	NORTH	EAST	SOUTH
1NT	Double	2♡	2♠
No	4♠	end	

Your opener showed 13–15; all other bids were natural.

You lead the queen of hearts to dummy's king, partner's encouraging eight and declarer's three. Dummy's ten of clubs fetches partner's four, South's two and your jack. Your five of hearts loses to dummy's ace, partner playing the two and South the seven. Now the three of diamonds is led. Partner plays the two, South the six and you win. How do you continue?

Provided you play a club or trump (probably safer) at this point, declarer must go down but with which card did you win that diamond trick? If the seven, you have killed the defence. Did you try to count four tricks for your side? One club you have. Partner's two of diamonds suggests a balanced suit distribution so two tricks are there. You will clearly not make a trick in trumps so you must hope South started with three small hearts. South threatens to set up his fourth diamond for a discard and you must make East win a trick in the suit. So you must keep that precious seven. You should have won the diamond trick with an honour and be prepared to throw the other under the ace, playing partner for ◇ Q 9 2.

The deal:

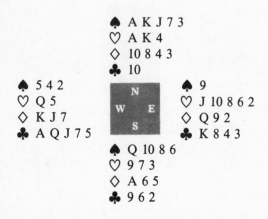

```
                    ♠ A K J 7 3
                    ♡ A K 4
                    ◇ 10 8 4 3
                    ♣ 10
 ♠ 5 4 2                              ♠ 9
 ♡ Q 5              N                 ♡ J 10 8 6 2
 ◇ K J 7         W     E              ◇ Q 9 2
 ♣ A Q J 7 5        S                 ♣ K 8 4 3
                    ♠ Q 10 8 6
                    ♡ 9 7 3
                    ◇ A 6 5
                    ♣ 9 6 2
```

When this hand appeared in a major national event, I was North and two points about my partner's excellent declarer play are noteworthy. Firstly, West's failure to lead a club suggested a broken holding in the suit implying that East may well have the king. This would be a possible entry to the winning heart and that line of communication had to be cut in time. Secondly, he did not touch trumps. This was partly to give the impression of a cross-ruff and thus to mask the true position, but more important, two rounds of trumps might have given East a chance to discard a low club, indicating an interest in diamonds after which the correct defence is much easier to find. He got home against two international champions and after West had won that diamond trick with the seven, East gave a generous lecture on the subject of meanness!

HAND 13
Dealer North
Game all

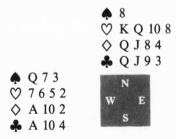

```
              ♠ 8
              ♡ K Q 10 8
              ◇ Q J 8 4
              ♣ Q J 9 3
  ♠ Q 7 3         N
  ♡ 7 6 5 2    W     E
  ◇ A 10 2        S
  ♣ A 10 4
```

The Bidding

WEST	NORTH	EAST	SOUTH
	1◇	No	1♠
No	1NT	No	2♠
end			

With so many queens and jacks, I would be reluctant to open an 11–15, 1◇ on the North cards, but we are not here to criticise opponents' bidding.

You lead the six of hearts to dummy's eight, partner's nine and South's ace. He now plays the two of clubs; plan your defence.

The magic question revolves around South's heart holding; how many has he? If he has four, he might well have bid them. If he has three, you are probably not going to beat this contract; in any case you will gain nothing by playing low to this trick. If he has two, he surely would have taken an immediate discard. The critical case arises where that ace is a singleton and South has the king of clubs. Now ducking is fatal. You must take your ace and play the ace of diamonds, prepared to lead another one if partner encourages. After that, you can relax and wait for any trump tricks available.

The deal:

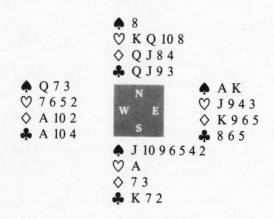

```
                    ♠ 8
                    ♡ K Q 10 8
                    ◇ Q J 8 4
                    ♣ Q J 9 3
  ♠ Q 7 3               N            ♠ A K
  ♡ 7 6 5 2         W       E        ♡ J 9 4 3
  ◇ A 10 2              S            ◇ K 9 6 5
  ♣ A 10 4                           ♣ 8 6 5
                    ♠ J 10 9 6 5 4 2
                    ♡ A
                    ◇ 7 3
                    ♣ K 7 2
```

HAND 14
Dealer South
N–S Vulnerable

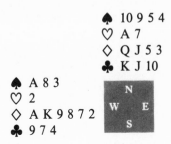

♠ 10 9 5 4
♡ A 7
◇ Q J 5 3
♣ K J 10

♠ A 8 3
♡ 2
◇ A K 9 8 7 2
♣ 9 7 4

The Bidding

SOUTH	WEST	NORTH	EAST
1♡	2◇	Double	No
3♠	No	4♠	end

North's double was negative and South's bidding showed 14–15 with at least five hearts and four spades.

You lead the ace of diamonds to the three, ten and four. How do you continue?

This hand could hardly be easier and yet when it came up in the qualifying round of a big national tournament, a quite well-known player went wrong. Your partner's ten of diamonds could be singleton or doubleton but the important point to realise is that even if declarer has the singleton and your king of diamonds is ruffed and dummy's two honours are set up, it is unlikely to cost; while failure to cash your honour may be fatal if South is 4–5–2–2.

The deal:

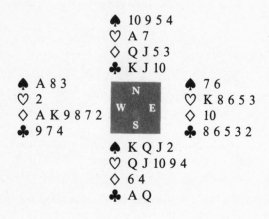

```
                    ♠ 10 9 5 4
                    ♡ A 7
                    ◇ Q J 5 3
                    ♣ K J 10
    ♠ A 8 3                          ♠ 7 6
    ♡ 2                              ♡ K 8 6 5 3
    ◇ A K 9 8 7 2                    ◇ 10
    ♣ 9 7 4                          ♣ 8 6 5 3 2
                    ♠ K Q J 2
                    ♡ Q J 10 9 4
                    ◇ 6 4
                    ♣ A Q
```

HAND 15
Dealer West
E–W Vulnerable

♠ A K J 7 6 2
♡ —
♢ Q 9 5 3
♣ A Q 6

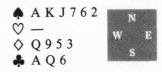

The Bidding

WEST	NORTH	EAST	SOUTH
1♣	No	1♠	2♡
2♠	3♡	4♢	No
6♠	No	No	Double
No	7♡	No	No
Double	end		

After your 16 plus opener, your partner's reply showed 8–10, balanced. His 4♢ bid agreed spades and showed the ace of diamonds, denying the ace of clubs. Meanwhile, opponents set up a possible sacrifice situation by agreeing hearts and South's double of the slam indicated one defensive trick. North obviously could not find another one. What do you lead?

It is clear that any tricks available to declarer will be in trumps and it should be your aim to cut down ruffs to a minimum by drawing them as soon as possible. It is, of course, impossible to do this from your side and you must try to get partner in. The bidding clearly indicates a diamond lead.

The deal:

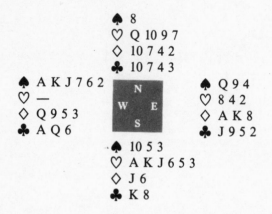

```
                    ♠ 8
                    ♡ Q 10 9 7
                    ◇ 10 7 4 2
                    ♣ 10 7 4 3
♠ A K J 7 6 2          N           ♠ Q 9 4
♡ —                 W     E        ♡ 8 4 2
◇ Q 9 5 3                          ◇ A K 8
♣ A Q 6                S           ♣ J 9 5 2
                    ♠ 10 5 3
                    ♡ A K J 6 5 3
                    ◇ J 6
                    ♣ K 8
```

The lead of either black suit gives up at least one unnecessary trick.

HAND 16
Dealer North
Love all

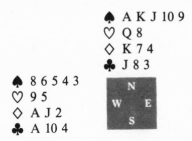

                    ♠ A K J 10 9
                    ♡ Q 8
                    ◇ K 7 4
                    ♣ J 8 3
    ♠ 8 6 5 4 3
    ♡ 9 5
    ◇ A J 2
    ♣ A 10 4

The Bidding

WEST	NORTH	EAST	SOUTH
	1♠	No	2NT
No	3NT	end	

An Acol sequence with South showing 11–12.

You lead the nine of hearts to the queen, king and three. Partner continues with the jack and South wins with the ace. He now plays the three of diamonds to the two, king and six and continues with the seven of diamonds to partner's eight and his ten; plan your defence.

You certainly have hit the jackpot with your opening lead. South's lack of interest in the spade suit clearly marks him with the queen and he must surely have the queen of diamonds. That totals eight points so far and you can see that he has five spade tricks and will make two diamond tricks to add up to eight, counting the ace of hearts. This means that you will need to find him with the king of clubs and partner with the queen. If you take the jack of diamonds now and exit with a spade, dummy's spades will be cleared and then a third diamond will be played to your ace leaving you to open up the clubs presenting declarer with his ninth trick. To avoid this, you must cash both your diamonds now before the spade exit and you cannot now be embarrassed. Did you notice declarer's blind spot? The heart position was clear which implied that both minor aces had to be in your hand. He thought that he would have to keep the queen of spades intact as the only possible entry to the fourth diamond but this does not stand close analysis. He should have run all the spades before the second diamond, leaving you helpless. Hopefully, you made him pay for his error.

The deal:

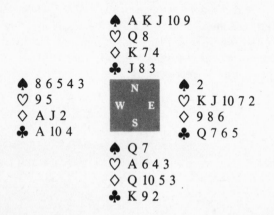

HAND 17

Dealer South
E–W Vulnerable

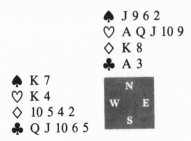

```
                          ♠ J 9 6 2
                          ♡ A Q J 10 9
                          ◇ K 8
                          ♣ A 3
         ♠ K 7            ┌─────────┐
         ♡ K 4            │    N    │
         ◇ 10 5 4 2       │  W   E  │
         ♣ Q J 10 6 5     │    S    │
                          └─────────┘
```

The Bidding

SOUTH	WEST	NORTH	EAST
1NT	No	2◇	No
3♡	No	4♣	No
4◇	No	4♡	No
4♠	No	6♡	end

After the 12–14 1NT, North transferred to hearts and South
with a maximum and four trumps, bid one extra. Cue-bidding
followed.

You lead the queen of clubs to the three, two and king.
Declarer leads a low heart to the nine and returns to hand with
the ace of spades to repeat the finesse. Dummy captures your
king, partner following. The ace of clubs is cashed and the eight
of diamonds is led to South's queen, partner playing the seven
and declarer ruffs his last club in dummy, partner following.
The king of diamonds is now led. Partner plays the three and
South overtakes. He cashes the jack of diamonds, discarding a
spade and exits with the four of spades; plan your defence.

The crucial moment in the play came at trick three. When declarer returned to hand with the ace of spades, did you perform a roll-call on the spade-suit and then ask the magic question? Clearly, if South had the queen of spades, he would have had no reason to reject the finesse so that card must be with East. Similarly, how about the ten? Again, if South had it, he would have played it rather than the ace in case partner had both honours or doubleton or trebleton with one. In any of those contingencies, another spade trick could be set up. So that too must be with East. You thus should have realised that it could not possibly cost to throw your king under the ace and that it could well be suicidal not to do so. If you are still holding him now, you are obliged to win and give a ruff and discard.

The deal:

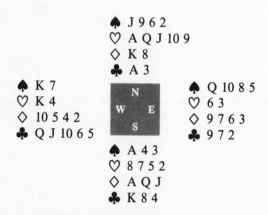

```
                ♠ J 9 6 2
                ♡ A Q J 10 9
                ◇ K 8
                ♣ A 3
♠ K 7                           ♠ Q 10 8 5
♡ K 4           N               ♡ 6 3
◇ 10 5 4 2   W     E            ◇ 9 7 6 3
♣ Q J 10 6 5    S               ♣ 9 7 2
                ♠ A 4 3
                ♡ 8 7 5 2
                ◇ A Q J
                ♣ K 8 4
```

The bidding was, of course, atrocious. South had little right to go beyond game and North should have tried 5 ◇ before committing the pair to a slam. Having said that, far crazier things have happened, even in top-class circles, and with the trump finesse right, this contract would be a success against all but the most alert defenders.

HAND 18

Dealer West
Game all

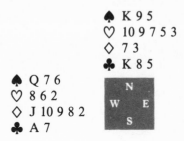

                    ♠ K 9 5
                    ♡ 10 9 7 5 3
                    ◇ 7 3
                    ♣ K 8 5
    ♠ Q 7 6
    ♡ 8 6 2
    ◇ J 10 9 8 2
    ♣ A 7

The Bidding

WEST	NORTH	EAST	SOUTH
No	No	No	1♡
No	2♡	No	2NT
No	4♡	end	

The 2NT showed 17–18.

You lead the jack of diamonds to the three, ace and four. Partner cashes the ace of trumps and then leads the queen of diamonds. South wins and plays the jack of clubs; plan your defence.

Did you duck this trick nice and smoothly to give South a chance to go wrong? If you did, then I am afraid you have killed the defence, having failed to do a points roll-call or ask yourself the magic question in respect of both your partner's defence and South's play. Partner produced ten points on the first three tricks leaving South with the rest – including the queen of clubs. So why the jack? Also, what was partner's reason for the hurry to cash the ace of trumps?

The deal:

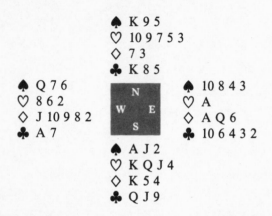

```
              ♠ K 9 5
              ♡ 10 9 7 5 3
              ◇ 7 3
              ♣ K 8 5
♠ Q 7 6                        ♠ 10 8 4 3
♡ 8 6 2           N            ♡ A
◇ J 10 9 8 2    W   E          ◇ A Q 6
♣ A 7             S            ♣ 10 6 4 3 2
              ♠ A J 2
              ♡ K Q J 4
              ◇ K 5 4
              ♣ Q J 9
```

The ace of trumps, as you well know from the bidding, was a singleton. East used a bit of foresight. If he played the queen of diamonds at once, South could eliminate the suit and then play a trump forcing East to open up a black suit with possibly fatal results if he picked the wrong one; for example if South's clubs were A J 9 he could take two finesses in the suit, the first one being on the house. By cashing the heart ace, he kept himself out of trouble. Similarly, if you duck the club, trumps will be cleared, diamonds eliminated and you will be in on the second club obliged to give a ruff and discard or save declarer the spade finesse. A friend of mine was caught like that three times in one weekend congress – worthwhile if he remembers!

PART 2 DECLARER PLAY BY SOUTH

HAND 19
Dealer North
N–S Vulnerable

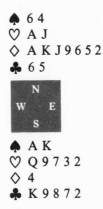

♠ 6 4
♡ A J
◇ A K J 9 6 5 2
♣ 6 5

♠ A K
♡ Q 9 7 3 2
◇ 4
♣ K 9 8 7 2

The Bidding

WEST	NORTH	EAST	SOUTH
	1◇	No	1♡
No	3◇	No	3NT
end			

North's rebid showed, in principle, 14–15 with a good five-card or longer diamond suit.

West leads the queen of spades; plan the play.

This is one of my favourite hard-luck stories. A similar hand to this came up in a cup match and not knowing the correct play, I took my time to work it out while my opponents waited patiently. Their patience was to be well rewarded. With three top tricks in the majors, I needed six in diamonds. If they broke three-two, no problem. Five-nil: no chance. Four-one: if East had Q 10 x x, no chance. If West had four, I had to go up if East's singleton was an honour but finesse if it was small. The odds 60–40, favoured the finesse; but the nine or the jack?

If East had a lone honour, it was just as likely to be the ten as the queen. The jack, however, gives the overtrick if West has Q x x. Satisfied that I had worked it out correctly, I duly lost to a singleton queen. The hand collapsed; 11 i.m.p. away and we lost the match by that margin. Here, you win if you played either nine or jack.

The deal:

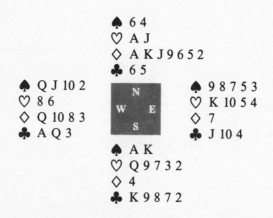

♠ 6 4
♥ A J
♦ A K J 9 6 5 2
♣ 6 5

♠ Q J 10 2
♥ 8 6
♦ Q 10 8 3
♣ A Q 3

♠ 9 8 7 5 3
♥ K 10 5 4
♦ 7
♣ J 10 4

♠ A K
♥ Q 9 7 3 2
♦ 4
♣ K 9 8 7 2

HAND 20
Dealer East
E–W Vulnerable

♠ 6 4 2
♡ A 5 2
◇ K 6 3
♣ K 10 4 2

♠ K Q 7 3
♡ K Q J 9 6
◇ 8 7
♣ A 5

The Bidding

WEST	NORTH	EAST	SOUTH
		No	1♡
Double	1NT	No	4♡
end			

After your 11–15 opening (5 card major), North's bid over the double showed a good balanced raise to 2♡.

West leads the eight of hearts; plan the play.

The bidding suggests that the two missing aces are with West and he is likely to have four spades. Your fourth spade will, therefore, have to be ruffed so West must not have more than two trumps (else he draws three rounds) and your ruff will have to be with the ace of trumps otherwise East overruffs. Win the lead in hand and play the king of spades, West wins (nothing to gain by not doing so) and plays another trump. Win again in hand and cross to the king of clubs to play a second spade. (This is a point of technique against a singleton spade with East, unnecessary as the cards lie. The singleton implies that you could have been defeated at the start by a spade lead.) When the queen of spades holds, play a third one and later ruff the fourth.

The deal:

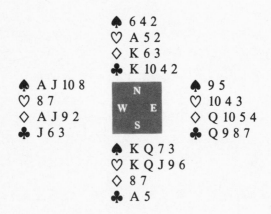

HAND 21
Dealer South
Game all

```
            ♠ A K 6 3
            ♡ Q 8 7 2
            ◇ 2
            ♣ A Q 9 8
                 N
            W         E
                 S
            ♠ Q J 5
            ♡ A K 6
            ◇ K 6 5 3
            ♣ 10 7 3
```

The Bidding

SOUTH	WEST	NORTH	EAST
1NT	No	2♣	No
2◇	No	3NT	end

A Stayman sequence followed your 13–15 opening.

West leads the ten of spades, your queen winning. You play the ace of hearts on which West discards the two of clubs, indicating an interest in diamonds. How do you play?

With eight top tricks and the king of diamonds likely to be badly placed, it appears that the club finesse will have to be right. However, it costs nothing to guard against a singleton king with East. Play the ace first and lead towards the queen later.

The deal:

```
                    ♠ A K 6 3
                    ♡ Q 8 7 2
                    ◇ 2
                    ♣ A Q 9 8
    ♠ 10 9 8 7                      ♠ 4 2
    ♡ —              N              ♡ J 10 9 5 4 3
    ◇ A 10 7 4    W     E           ◇ Q J 9 8
    ♣ J 6 5 4 2       S             ♣ K
                    ♠ Q J 5
                    ♡ A K 6
                    ◇ K 6 5 3
                    ♣ 10 7 3
```

Note West's choice of lead. Knowing that the cards were probably lying badly for you, he went for the solid, rather than the long-suit, lead.

HAND 22
Dealer West
Love all

```
              ♠ 9 2
              ♡ A 10 8 4
              ◇ A K J 7 4
              ♣ A K

              N
           W     E
              S

              ♠ K J 7
              ♡ K 6 2
              ◇ 9 8 2
              ♣ 9 5 3 2
```

The Bidding

WEST	NORTH	EAST	SOUTH
No	1♣	No	1◇
No	2◇	No	2NT
No	3♡	No	3NT
end			

After your partner's strong opening and your negative response, natural bidding followed.

West leads the four of spades to dummy's two and East's queen; plan the play.

The opening lead suggests that the ace of spades is with West and that the suit is breaking four-four or five-three. There is, therefore, no advantage in ducking and indeed winning trick one gives you a chance for a second stop provided East can be kept off play. Thus it is advisable to spurn the diamond finesse and play the ace and king. If both opponents follow and the queen fails to appear, play a third round hoping West will win. If he doesn't, bad luck.

The deal:

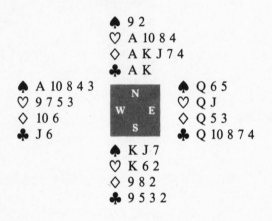

```
              ♠ 9 2
              ♡ A 10 8 4
              ◇ A K J 7 4
              ♣ A K
♠ A 10 8 4 3              ♠ Q 6 5
♡ 9 7 5 3      N          ♡ Q J
◇ 10 6      W   E         ◇ Q 5 3
♣ J 6          S          ♣ Q 10 8 7 4
              ♠ K J 7
              ♡ K 6 2
              ◇ 9 8 2
              ♣ 9 5 3 2
```

No – it isn't bad luck; it's bad play! Did you play the ace of hearts followed (if an honour drops) by the king in case there was a miracle in the suit before committing yourself to that third round of diamonds? Nine tricks are there if you did, although you will have to be prepared to congratulate East if he follows high twice from ♡QJ9.

HAND 23
Dealer North
E–W Vulnerable

<pre>
              ♠ 6 3 2
              ♡ Q 10 4
              ◇ A K 5
              ♣ K 9 5 2
                   N
               W   E
                   S
              ♠ A K 8 5 4
              ♡ J
              ◇ 9 7 6 2
              ♣ A 4 3
</pre>

The Bidding

WEST	NORTH	EAST	SOUTH
	1◇	1♡	2♠
No	3♠	No	4♠
end			

Your 2♠ bid was forcing for one round.

West leads the six of hearts to East's king. He now plays the queen of trumps; plan the play.

Unless the trumps break, you are not going to be successful so you should assume they do. Now you must look at the diamond suit. If it splits 3–3, there will be no problem. A 4–2 break implies that your fourth card must be ruffed in dummy at a stage when the defence can do no damage even if the shortage in spades and diamonds is in the same hand. This contract is thus an exercise in timing. You must win this trump trick and duck a diamond at once. On regaining the lead, you cash the other high trump, the two high diamonds and establish a heart trick by a ruffing finesse against East. You can ruff the fourth diamond in dummy and concede the outstanding trump having discarded your club loser on the established heart.

The deal:

```
              ♠ 6 3 2
              ♡ Q 10 4
              ◇ A K 5
              ♣ K 9 5 2
  ♠ 9 7          N          ♠ Q J 10
  ♡ 7 6 5 3   W     E       ♡ A K 9 8 2
  ◇ 10 3         S          ◇ Q J 8 4
  ♣ J 10 8 7 6             ♣ Q
              ♠ A K 8 5 4
              ♡ J
              ◇ 9 7 6 2
              ♣ A 4 3
```

When this hand appeared in a match for mixed teams, 470 points changed hands when the winning line was found in one room only. The fact the successful declarer finished up on the losing side by nearly 4000 is neither here nor there!

HAND 24
Dealer East
Game all

♠ Q 9 5
♥ K Q 8 3
♦ A 5 3 2
♣ K 6

♠ A J 10 7 6 2
♥ 10 5
♦ Q J 4
♣ A 7

The Bidding

WEST	NORTH	EAST	SOUTH
		No	1♠
No	2♦	No	2♠
No	4♠	end	

Your bidding showed 11–13 and almost certainly six spades.

West leads the ten of diamonds; plan the play.

This is very much a study in percentages and I think, particularly as the lead indicates that the king of diamonds is likely to be with East, that your best chance is to reject both the finesses. Win the first trick and play ace and another trump. You will then be unlucky to go down where other lines would have worked better.

The deal:

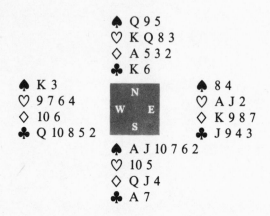

```
                 ♠ Q 9 5
                 ♡ K Q 8 3
                 ◇ A 5 3 2
                 ♣ K 6
   ♠ K 3                          ♠ 8 4
   ♡ 9 7 6 4        N             ♡ A J 2
   ◇ 10 6       W       E         ◇ K 9 8 7
   ♣ Q 10 8 5 2     S             ♣ J 9 4 3
                 ♠ A J 10 7 6 2
                 ♡ 10 5
                 ◇ Q J 4
                 ♣ A 7
```

As the cards lie, you can still succeed even if you do take the diamond finesse as long as you do not also take the trump finesse; play ace and another.

HAND 25
Dealer South
Love all

♠ Q 5 4 3
♥ Q 10 8 6
♦ K J 9
♣ J 9

♠ A K 7
♥ 7
♦ A 6 3 2
♣ A K 10 8 7

The Bidding

SOUTH	WEST	NORTH	EAST
1♣	No	1♠	No
1NT	No	2♥	No
3NT	end		

After your Precision 16–plus opening, North's reply showed
8–10, balanced. Your 1NT asked for more information.

West leads the two of spades; plan the play.

[63]

Even if you lose one club trick, you have enough tricks for the contract. The danger lies in hearts and four tricks may be available to the defence if the first lead comes from West. If East has to start the opponents' attack, they can never take more than three. You should therefore aim to keep West off play by rejecting the club finesse and playing the suit from the top.

The deal:

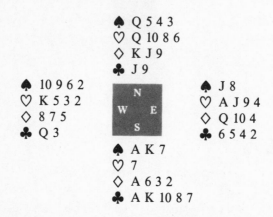

```
                    ♠ Q 5 4 3
                    ♡ Q 10 8 6
                    ◇ K J 9
                    ♣ J 9
  ♠ 10 9 6 2                        ♠ J 8
  ♡ K 5 3 2          N              ♡ A J 9 4
  ◇ 8 7 5        W       E          ◇ Q 10 4
  ♣ Q 3              S              ♣ 6 5 4 2
                    ♠ A K 7
                    ♡ 7
                    ◇ A 6 3 2
                    ♣ A K 10 8 7
```

You could try the diamond finesse early but if that fails, you will have to bring in clubs without loss even if the defence takes three heart tricks only. The best chance would then be surely to finesse, failing as the cards lie. Even if the diamond finesse succeeds, you will have to decide whether to play the ace and king to test the split, risking setting up the queen of diamonds for West. Again, the clubs will have to be brought in free of charge even if the defence has three heart tricks only.

HAND 26
Dealer West
N–S Vulnerable

```
                    ♠ K Q 10 9 8
                    ♡ K 7 6 2
                    ◇ 6
                    ♣ K J 2
                   ┌─────────┐
                   │    N    │
                   │ W     E │
                   │    S    │
                   └─────────┘
                    ♠ A J 5
                    ♡ Q 10
                    ◇ Q 9 8 5 3
                    ♣ Q 6 4
```

The Bidding

WEST	NORTH	EAST	SOUTH
1NT	2◇	No	3♣
No	3♡	No	4♠
end			

After the 12–14 1NT opener, the 2◇ bid showed an opening bid with at least nine cards in spades and another suit. Your 3♣ bid was positive and asked partner to name his other suit. Your 4♠ bid can only be described as highly optimistic.

West leads the four of spades; plan the play.

[65]

As always in a hand that has been blatantly overbid, you must assume that the opposing cards are well placed for you, bearing in mind – just as important – that your assumptions must be consistent with the bidding. The trump lead is awkward and your ability to ruff dummy's low hearts is threatened. You will need to find the jack of hearts with East and both club and heart aces with West. Further, he must have exactly two spades and three diamonds. Even so, playing on hearts now will fail. West will win and play his second trump. You can cash your heart queen but will not be able to return to dummy without letting West in, and he can now cross to his partner in diamonds after which the third trump will be fatal for you. Accordingly, you must play diamonds immediately: the heart finesse must wait. Even if the defence forces you with diamonds, the fact that West has only three saves you from losing control.

The deal:

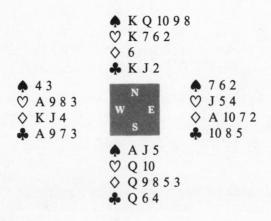

```
                    ♠ K Q 10 9 8
                    ♡ K 7 6 2
                    ◇ 6
                    ♣ K J 2
    ♠ 4 3                              ♠ 7 6 2
    ♡ A 9 8 3          N              ♡ J 5 4
    ◇ K J 4        W       E          ◇ A 10 7 2
    ♣ A 9 7 3          S              ♣ 10 8 5
                    ♠ A J 5
                    ♡ Q 10
                    ◇ Q 9 8 5 3
                    ♣ Q 6 4
```

HAND 27
Dealer North
Game all

```
              ♠ A K 4 2
              ♡ 6 5
              ◇ Q 9 7 4 3
              ♣ 8 5
```

```
              ♠ 6 5 3
              ♡ A K Q J 9 8
              ◇ A
              ♣ Q 7 6
```

The Bidding

WEST	NORTH	EAST	SOUTH
	No	No	1♣
No	2◇	No	2♡
No	2♠	No	3♣
No	3♡	No	4♡
end			

Another 16 plus opener was followed by 2◇, showing 8–10 with 5 plus diamonds. South's 3♣ suggested 3NT if North could help stop clubs.

West leads the two of hearts to his partner's ten; plan the play.

Again the trump lead has threatened your ability to win by ruffing and it looks as though, with seven top tricks in your hand, the other three will have to come from spades. For this to materialise, you must duck a spade at once to keep control. Note that if you cash one honour and then duck, the defence can play the third round immediately and dummy is dead. There is, however, one small extra chance. The king of diamonds may be singleton or doubleton. To cater for this, you should cash your ace now and then duck the spade. As you will see, delaying this play is no good.

The deal:

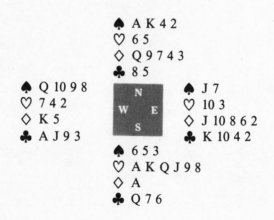

```
              ♠ A K 4 2
              ♡ 6 5
              ◇ Q 9 7 4 3
              ♣ 8 5
♠ Q 10 9 8                  ♠ J 7
♡ 7 4 2         N           ♡ 10 3
◇ K 5        W   E          ◇ J 10 8 6 2
♣ A J 9 3       S           ♣ K 10 4 2
              ♠ 6 5 3
              ♡ A K Q J 9 8
              ◇ A
              ♣ Q 7 6
```

HAND 28
Dealer East
Love all

```
              ♠ A Q 8 6 3
              ♡ K J
              ◊ K J 10 3
              ♣ K 7
                  ┌─────────┐
                  │    N    │
                  │  W   E  │
                  │    S    │
                  └─────────┘
              ♠ 10 5 2
              ♡ A 9 8 7 4
              ◊ A Q 8
              ♣ A J
```

The Bidding

WEST	NORTH	EAST	SOUTH
		No	1 ♡
No	1 ♠	No	2NT
No	6NT	end	

West leads the ten of clubs to the seven, two and jack. You play a low spade to the four, queen and seven. How do you continue?

This could hardly be simpler. You need four spade tricks for the contract and with the finesse right, a three-two break will suffice. If they are four-one, you will have to try the hearts. You must take the ace of spades next to see what is required. Don't do what I did and try to 'keep control' by ducking the second spade; you now lose a considerable proportion of your chance in the other major.

I tell this story against myself deliberately to illustrate how easy it is to have a blind spot in a perfectly simple hand.

The deal:

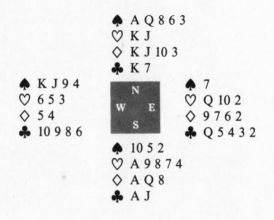

HAND 29
Dealer South
N–S Vulnerable

♠ A Q J 10 9
♡ 6 4
◇ A Q 10 3 2
♣ 5

♠ K 8 7
♡ A 5
◇ K 6 4
♣ A J 10 9 6

The Bidding

SOUTH	WEST	NORTH	EAST
1NT	No	2♡	No
2♠	No	3◇	No
3♡	No	4◇	No
4♡	No	4♠	No
5♣	No	6◇	No
6♠	end		

After your 13–15 1NT, partner transferred to spades and showed a diamond suit with 11 plus, forcing to 3♠ at least. Your 3♡ bid was a waiting move, possibly to become an advanced cue-bid if North was slam-minded. North now showed a five-card diamond suit and cue-bids followed.

West leads the nine of hearts on which East plays the ten; plan the play.

There will be twelve tricks on top if the diamonds break or East has the singleton. But if he has J9xx, you will have to look elsewhere. Nothing is lost, therefore, by trying clubs first. Win the heart lead and cash the ace of clubs. Follow with the jack, discarding dummy's losing heart if West does not cover. You have the king of trumps as entry to your hand to repeat the process, ruffing regardless. Extra club tricks will be established if both honours fall in three rounds or if West has both in any reasonable distribution. Note that even if West covers twice, you will probably only fail if he also has four trumps and a singleton or void diamond. If the club play does not work, clear trumps and play the ace of diamonds followed by the king to prepare to take the marked finesse against West should East show out.

The deal:

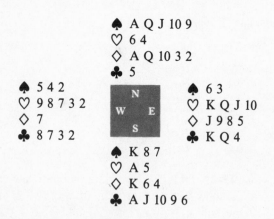

```
                    ♠ A Q J 10 9
                    ♡ 6 4
                    ◇ A Q 10 3 2
                    ♣ 5
     ♠ 5 4 2          N            ♠ 6 3
     ♡ 9 8 7 3 2                   ♡ K Q J 10
     ◇ 7          W       E        ◇ J 9 8 5
     ♣ 8 7 3 2        S            ♣ K Q 4
                    ♠ K 8 7
                    ♡ A 5
                    ◇ K 6 4
                    ♣ A J 10 9 6
```

HAND 30
Dealer West
E–W Vulnerable

```
              ♠ 6 5 4 2
              ♡ J 7
              ◇ K 9 2
              ♣ J 8 7 3
                 ┌─────┐
                 │  N  │
                 │W   E│
                 │  S  │
                 └─────┘
              ♠ A K 10 9 7
              ♡ A K
              ◇ 6 4
              ♣ A Q 4 2
```

The Bidding

WEST	NORTH	EAST	SOUTH
No	No	No	1♣
No	1◇	No	1♠
No	2♠	No	4♠
end			

After your strong 1♣ and negative response, natural bidding followed.

West leads the queen of diamonds. You correctly take the view that he would not lead from the ace to your strong hand and you therefore play low. East encourages and two more rounds follow. You ruff East's ace and draw trumps in two rounds. How do you continue?

With two diamond tricks already lost, the object must be to avoid two club losers. If the suit breaks 3-2, there is no problem. You must guard against K 109 x or K 109 x x in one hand. It is most unlikely that West has a singleton as he did not lead it, or switch to it, when he had the chance. You can protect against a singleton or void with East by cashing the two hearts and then leading low towards dummy's jack, ducking completely on the way back if it holds. This line is not 100%, however, as I discovered when I played the hand.

The deal:

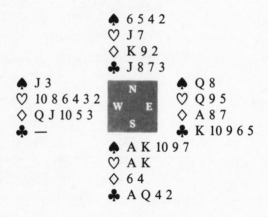

```
              ♠ 6 5 4 2
              ♡ J 7
              ♦ K 9 2
              ♣ J 8 7 3
♠ J 3                         ♠ Q 8
♡ 10 8 6 4 3 2                ♡ Q 9 5
♦ Q J 10 5 3                  ♦ A 8 7
♣ —                          ♣ K 10 9 6 5
              ♠ A K 10 9 7
              ♡ A K
              ♦ 6 4
              ♣ A Q 4 2
```

The safe line, which I sadly overlooked, is to cash the hearts and lead the queen of clubs from hand, intending to play low from both hands on the next round if it holds. No lie of the cards can now beat you. Note the importance of refraining from playing the king of diamonds to either of the first two tricks. If you put it on, East has the chance to give his partner a ruff without ruining his own natural club trick.

HAND 31
Dealer North
Love all

```
              ♠ K 7 5
              ♡ 9 8 6 3
              ◇ 8 2
              ♣ K Q 9 8
```

```
              ♠ A Q 4 2
              ♡ J
              ◇ K Q 3
              ♣ A 7 6 5 2
```

The Bidding

WEST	NORTH	EAST	SOUTH
	No	1◇	Double
No	2♡	No	3NT
end			

We could spend hours discussing what you should bid over 1◇. There is a case for the double, 1NT, 2♣ or perhaps even a pass. None is entirely satisfactory. North's reply showed about 8–10, non-forcing and once again you have pushed a bit, having upvalued your diamond holding.

West leads the seven of diamonds. East wins with the ace and continues the suit with the jack; plan the play.

You will have to bring the club suit in to make this contract. If West is void, there is nothing to be done but if East has the blank, you can capture West's holding provided you start with the ace. That way, you can take five club tricks, three spade tricks (assuming they don't break) and one diamond. Yes – that's right – just one. You did, of course, throw your queen on trick one to give yourself the best chance of getting that diamond continuation. If you didn't, then East asked himself whether there was any hope of a set unless quick heart tricks were available, decided that there wasn't and switched accordingly.

The deal:

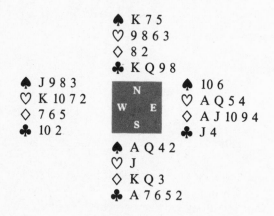

```
                    ♠ K 7 5
                    ♡ 9 8 6 3
                    ◇ 8 2
                    ♣ K Q 9 8
   ♠ J 9 8 3           N           ♠ 10 6
   ♡ K 10 7 2      W       E       ♡ A Q 5 4
   ◇ 7 6 5             S           ◇ A J 10 9 4
   ♣ 10 2                          ♣ J 4
                    ♠ A Q 4 2
                    ♡ J
                    ◇ K Q 3
                    ♣ A 7 6 5 2
```

With the clubs well-behaved, the safety play is unnecessary but you ought to have found it. The deception at trick one was found by a team-mate of mine in a mixed team competition. A top-class player in the East position duly sat on the porcupine.

HAND 32
Dealer East
N–S Vulnerable

♠ 10 5 3 2
♡ K Q J 5
♢ J 5 4
♣ 5 4

♠ K 8 4
♡ A 9 2
♢ A K Q
♣ K J 6 2

The Bidding

WEST	NORTH	EAST	SOUTH
		No	1♣
2♣	Double	No	3NT
end			

West's bid after your strong 1♣ showed at least nine cards in the minors. North's double promised 5–8 balanced.

West leads the seven of clubs to his partner's ace and East returns the nine; plan the play.

Many players bid on nothing against a strong 1♣ at this vulnerability but the odds favour the ace of spades being with West. In that case, you only have eight top tricks and your best chance for a ninth lies in a throw-in of the West hand. You must go up with the king of clubs and play your seven red suit winners ending in hand. Now you throw West in with one of the black suits dependent on his discards, on the assumption that he led his original longest suit and therefore started with five clubs.

The deal:

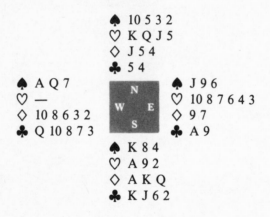

You can see that allowing the nine of clubs to hold permits a spade switch and playing the jack of clubs gives no chance. If West retains four diamonds on the hearts being played, he will either have to blank his ace of spades or queen of clubs in which case you can set up your ninth trick without having to clear all your diamonds.

HAND 33
Dealer South
E–W Vulnerable

♠ J 3
♡ J 5 4 2
◇ A 10 7 3
♣ 10 5 4

♠ A 8 7 5 4 2
♡ A Q 3
◇ K 6
♣ A K

The Bidding

SOUTH	WEST	NORTH	EAST
1♣	No	1◇	No
1♠	No	1NT	No
4♠	end		

After your strong 1♣ and a negative (less than 8) response, your 1♠ was natural and the 1NT showed 5–7, balanced.

West leads the two of diamonds; plan the play.

The shortage of entries to dummy makes this hand very awkward and the one entry you have got should be used with great care. You should notice that West has almost certainly led away from the queen of diamonds round to your announced strong hand which suggests that his holdings in other suits are as, or even more, unattractive. Extending this argument, you can observe that, with all the heart intermediates missing, you are only likely to avoid a loser in the suit by taking the finesse if East has precisely K9. The chance of this is less than 2% and even that assumes that West would prefer to lead from Qxxx against 10876. I suggest, therefore, that you accept a heart loser as inevitable and concentrate on avoiding three trump losers. If the suit breaks 3–2 or 5–0, there is nothing to discuss. You can protect against certain 4–1 splits by leading towards the jack and subsequently using your diamond entry to lead the second round from dummy with the intention of just covering East's card. The first trick therefore must be won in hand.

The deal:

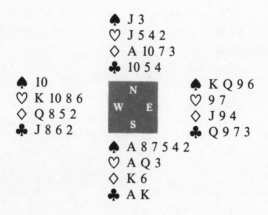

HAND 34
Dealer West
Game all

♠ K J 10
♡ K J 6
◇ K
♣ 8 6 5 4 3 2

♠ A 2
♡ A 10 8 5 4
◇ Q J 6
♣ A K Q

The Bidding

WEST	NORTH	EAST	SOUTH
No	No	No	1♣
No	2♣	No	2♡
No	3♡	No	3♠
No	4♡	No	5♣
No	6♡	end	

After your strong 1♣, the reply from North showed 8 plus with at least five clubs. Thereafter, hearts was agreed and cue-bidding followed.

Arguably, your 2♡ bid is ill-advised on the basis that one should not bid a weak suit when a slam is envisaged. Against this, if partner turns out to be absolutely minimal for his positive response, it may be a question of 4♡ or 5♣ with only the former making. Anyway, you must recover from the shock of seeing that 6♣ or 6NT are near certainties and try to make your actual contract.

West leads the nine of spades. You put on dummy's ten and East plays the three; plan the play.

With a diamond loser inevitable, the problem is to catch the queen of trumps. If the suit breaks 3–2, it's a toss up which way to finesse, although West's decision not to lead a trump swings the odds slightly his way. This is far outweighed by the ability to pick up the trumps if the queen is with East even if he has four. For that, you will need two entries to dummy and you must therefore win the first trick with the ace of spades, rejecting the free finesse which is of no worth anyway. Now cross to the king of trumps and run the jack, keeping the king of spades available for a further finesse in trumps if necessary.

The deal:

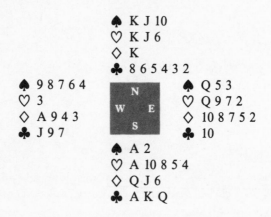

```
                    ♠ K J 10
                    ♡ K J 6
                    ◇ K
                    ♣ 8 6 5 4 3 2
    ♠ 9 8 7 6 4                    ♠ Q 5 3
    ♡ 3            N               ♡ Q 9 7 2
    ◇ A 9 4 3    W     E           ◇ 10 8 7 5 2
    ♣ J 9 7        S               ♣ 10
                    ♠ A 2
                    ♡ A 10 8 5 4
                    ◇ Q J 6
                    ♣ A K Q
```

HAND 35

Dealer North
N–S Vulnerable

```
              ♠ K Q 10 9 6
              ♡ A K Q
              ◇ Q
              ♣ J 9 7 6

                  N
              W       E
                  S

              ♠ 5 3
              ♡ J 9 6
              ◇ J 10 8 7
              ♣ A K 5 4
```

The Bidding

WEST	NORTH	EAST	SOUTH
	1♣	No	1♠
No	2♠	No	2NT
No	3NT	end	

The response to the strong 1♣ showed 8–10, balanced.

West leads the two of diamonds and your partner's queen holds as East follows with the six; plan the play.

The first thing to do here is to count your tricks. With one diamond already taken, three hearts and two clubs give you six. Thus only three spade tricks are required. Further, you do not mind losing tricks in the suit to West as he cannot profitably attack diamonds. The best line is thus to start spades immediately from the top, losing only if East has both honours with one or more extra cards and West's remaining diamonds are A K 9. If you cross to hand in clubs to lead spades towards dummy, you will allow the defence to set up a fifth trick by playing a second club when in with the first round of spades. This very difficult defence was, however, not found when I misplayed the hand originally.

The deal:

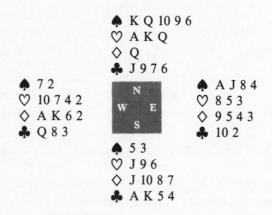

Dealer East
E–W Vulnerable

♠ 10 9 8
♡ Q 7 6 5 2
♦ K 2
♣ 9 4 3

```
        N
    W       E
        S
```

♠ A K 5 2
♡ A 4 3
♦ A 7 6 4
♣ A J

The Bidding

WEST	NORTH	EAST	SOUTH
		No	1♣
No	1♦	No	2NT
No	3♦	No	3♡
No	3NT	No	4♡
end			

After the strong 1♣ and negative response, your rebid showed 20–21, balanced. North's subsequent transfer sequence promised 5–7 with exactly five hearts and an otherwise balanced hand.

Your last bid has suggested ruffing values in your hand and it is no surprise when West leads the ten of trumps; plan the play.

East may have K J doubleton in hearts but if he has a third one you will have to lose two trump tricks as well as the obvious club. That means you will need to find both spade honours with East. Even now, careful timing is vital. Allow the ten of trumps to hold. Win the continuation with the ace and cross to the king of diamonds. East must be kept out of the lead so you have to lead clubs from dummy, putting in the jack when East plays low. Win the diamond return, cash the ace of clubs, ruff a diamond and lead the ten of spades. East does best to cover. You win, ruff your last diamond and lead the nine of spades. Note the club ruff must wait until the third spade has been established otherwise you will be an entry short. East does best to cover again and the eight of spades becomes entry for the club ruff.

The deal:

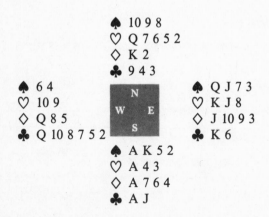

HAND 37
Dealer South
Game all

♠ A J 3
♡ 7 6 4
◇ Q J 2
♣ Q J 9 7

♠ K Q 5
♡ K J 5
◇ A K 5 3
♣ A K 8

The Bidding

SOUTH	WEST	NORTH	EAST
2NT	No	6NT	end

Your opening bid showed 22–23.

West leads the ten of spades; plan the play.

With eleven top tricks outside the heart suit, you will need a good guess to land your slam. If both the heart honours are in one hand, your line of play is of no interest. Note that you gain nothing by playing the jack when East has both honours as you can only take your second heart trick at 'trick 14'. Thus we must consider the possibility of split honours. It appears to be evenly balanced but in fact, the play of the king offers a small extra chance. Remember West cannot see your hand. He may therefore think you have ♡ K Q 10 x in which case, holding the ace, he must duck smoothly to give you a guess on the second round. You must not, however advertise the fact that you have the other suits solid and you are best to play hearts at trick two having won the first trick in dummy.

The deal:

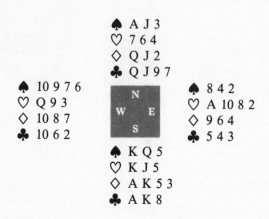

When this hand came up in a team of four match, the same contract was reached but with North as declarer. Now the heart position was on view for all to see and North was on a straight guess. He played the jack: one off. Unlucky, or was it?

Without knowing the lie of the cards and knowing that South might be declarer at another table in a team of four match, would you have played that way, preferred the king or mentally tossed a coin? The answer lies in considering the state of the match when the deal appears. If you are well ahead or about level, aim for a flat board by playing the king, realising this was the likely line for the other declarer. However, should the position heavily favour the opposing team, the hand would allow you to pull something back by going against that line of play.

HAND 38
Dealer West
Love all

```
              ♠ A Q J
              ♡ 8 7 4
              ◇ A J 4 2
              ♣ A Q J
                 ┌─────┐
                 │  N  │
                 │ W E │
                 │  S  │
                 └─────┘
              ♠ 10 8 4
              ♡ A K J
              ◇ K 8 5 3
              ♣ K 5 2
```

The Bidding

WEST	NORTH	EAST	SOUTH
No	1♣	No	3NT
No	6NT	end	

Your reply to the 16 plus opener showed 14–15, balanced.

West leads the ten of clubs; plan the play.

First look at the diamonds. K9xx opposite AJxx has appeared countless times to show a combination which provides three certain tricks by playing the ace first then low towards the king, covering whatever is put on, or if the next hand shows out, taking the king and leading towards the well-placed jack. Here you cannot guarantee three tricks but the safety play is still on if West's first card is the nine or ten. Before aiming for this, you must ensure that there are no losers in the majors. With hearts, you should play the ace first to guard against singleton queen with West and only then try the finesse. With spades, you simply take the finesse against West. If there are no losers, can you go for the diamonds as suggested? If that was your line of play, intending to play diamonds in the normal manner if you lost a major trick then you are nearly right – but not quite. When you tried that spade finesse, did you specifically say that you intended to take it twice? You must, because East ducked the first time in an attempt (unlikely to cost) to throw you off the rails. When the second finesse loses, you have to play West for Qx or Qxx in diamonds.

The deal:

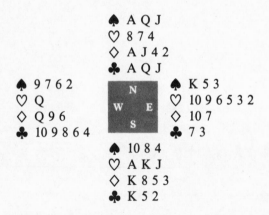

```
                 ♠ A Q J
                 ♡ 8 7 4
                 ◇ A J 4 2
                 ♣ A Q J
  ♠ 9 7 6 2                      ♠ K 5 3
  ♡ Q              N             ♡ 10 9 6 5 3 2
  ◇ Q 9 6      W       E         ◇ 10 7
  ♣ 10 9 8 6 4       S           ♣ 7 3
                 ♠ 10 8 4
                 ♡ A K J
                 ◇ K 8 5 3
                 ♣ K 5 2
```

Note an important point for the defenders. If South fails to take a second spade finesse and leads a low diamond towards the table, West should put in the nine to suggest that the safety play against ◇ Q 10xx with East may be available.

HAND 39
Dealer North
E–W Vulnerable

                    ♠ 10 9 6 2
                    ♡ A K Q 7
                    ♢ A K 6
                    ♣ 9 7

                    ┌─────────┐
                    │   N   │
                    │ W   E │
                    │   S   │
                    └─────────┘

                    ♠ Q J 8 7
                    ♡ J 9 8 6 5
                    ♢ 10 8
                    ♣ K 4

The Bidding

WEST	NORTH	EAST	SOUTH
	1♣	No	1♢
No	1NT	No	2♢
No	2♡	No	2♠
No	4♠	end	

North's 1♣ showed 16 up and after his partner's negative reply, the rebid promised 16–19, balanced. The 2♢ bid was a transfer to hearts, after which the bidding was natural.

West leads the jack of clubs and you are grateful to see that you will be losing only one trick in the suit rather than the statutory two you normally concede in these situations. You play the seven from dummy and East produces the queen. If ever there was a hand for the magic question, this is it. How do you plan the play?

The play seems strange. Has West presented you with an unmakeable contract by a lead from ♣ A J 10 x or the like, or has East withheld the ace for some reason? I think you should rule out the underlead, but if East has the ace why didn't he play it?

If you can get only that far, the whole hand becomes an open book. Let's ask another question – who has the ten of clubs? Surely West, else East has at least a seven-card suit which he would have bid and he certainly would not have ducked trick one. Is the fog beginning to clear? When you take your king now, the ten becomes an entry to the West hand. East must be desperate to create that entry in West's hand. Do you see what is happening? East must have both trump honours and at least one more trump together with a singleton heart. If you start drawing trumps now, he will win and play his heart. Winning the next trump, he will put his partner in with the ten of clubs and a heart ruff will set the game. To counter this, you must force the defence to use their entry prematurely by winning trick one and returning a club immediately. You will now be defeated only if East has at least four cards in both black suits.

The deal:

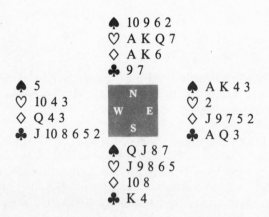

```
            ♠ 10 9 6 2
            ♡ A K Q 7
            ◇ A K 6
            ♣ 9 7
♠ 5                         ♠ A K 4 3
♡ 10 4 3          N        ♡ 2
◇ Q 4 3      W       E     ◇ J 9 7 5 2
♣ J 10 8 6 5 2     S       ♣ A Q 3
            ♠ Q J 8 7
            ♡ J 9 8 6 5
            ◇ 10 8
            ♣ K 4
```

When this hand came up, East produced the queen of clubs at trick one with little or no thought. South, a compulsive underleader of aces, thought it was his lucky day and promptly dived into the sharks.

HAND 40

Dealer East
Game all

```
              ♠ Q J 9 8
              ♡ K J 5
              ◇ A J 9 3
              ♣ 4 2

                   N
              W         E
                   S

              ♠ 10 7 3
              ♡ A 4
              ◇ 10 6 4
              ♣ A K Q J 10
```

The Bidding

WEST	NORTH	EAST	SOUTH
		No	1NT
No	2♣	No	2◇
No	3NT	end	

Your opener showed 13–15.

West leads the six of hearts; plan the play.

With eight top tricks, if you play on spades, you will only fail if West has both honours and East the queen of hearts – a 90% plus chance when you add the chance of a four-four or six-two heart split. Diamonds, however, offer an even bigger chance of success. Now, in addition to the above misfortunes, both diamond honours must be with East for the defence to prevail. You should play a diamond towards dummy at trick two.

The deal:

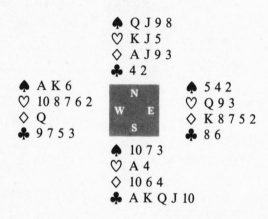

```
                    ♠ Q J 9 8
                    ♡ K J 5
                    ◇ A J 9 3
                    ♣ 4 2
    ♠ A K 6              N          ♠ 5 4 2
    ♡ 10 8 7 6 2                    ♡ Q 9 3
    ◇ Q           W         E       ◇ K 8 7 5 2
    ♣ 9 7 5 3              S        ♣ 8 6
                    ♠ 10 7 3
                    ♡ A 4
                    ◇ 10 6 4
                    ♣ A K Q J 10
```

As the cards lie, you are still successful if you rise with the king of hearts on the second round even if you do play on spades, but that is surely against the odds and I don't think you should do that in practice. When this hand came up in an important match, I played on spades. A world champion was in the corresponding seat at the other table. But . . . flat board!

HAND 41
Dealer South
Love all

```
            ♠ A Q 10 7 5
            ♡ 10 4
            ◇ K 5
            ♣ J 10 8 2

                N
            W       E
                S

            ♠ J 9 6 3
            ♡ K Q J 5
            ◇ A 9 2
            ♣ Q 4
```

The Bidding

SOUTH	WEST	NORTH	EAST
1NT	No	2♡	No
2♠	No	2NT	No
4♠	end		

After the 13–15 1NT and transfer to spades, North's 2NT strictly speaking, showed 11 points, exactly five spades and an otherwise balanced hand. He valued up his tens and decided to suppress the poor club suit.

West leads the seven of clubs to the two, ace and four. East returns the queen of diamonds; plan the play.

The magic question here applies to the play on trick one. Anything strange? Who has got the king of clubs? If it's West, he has led from ♣K 9 7 round to a 1NT – an unlikely lead. If it's East, he has deliberately false-carded and clearly does not want you to know that he has the king. Why not? There must be a link with other vital information. Continuing this train of thought, you can see that there are two possibilities. The most likely is that East started with A K x x x and West 7 x. In that case he must have a singleton king of spades – there can be no other reason for refusing to play three rounds of clubs. The other possibility, less likely on the lead, is that West started with ♣9 7 x x x and East with A K. To establish the truth, you should win the diamond in hand and play clubs yourself. If West does have the king, finesse in trumps normally. If East has it, win the next diamond and play a third club. If East shows out, finesse in trumps. If he follows, ruff high and all will be revealed.

The deal:

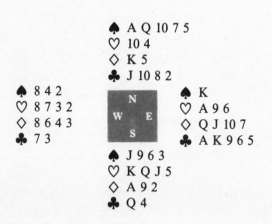

```
              ♠ A Q 10 7 5
              ♡ 10 4
              ♦ K 5
              ♣ J 10 8 2
♠ 8 4 2                        ♠ K
♡ 8 7 3 2          N           ♡ A 9 6
♦ 8 6 4 3      W       E       ♦ Q J 10 7
♣ 7 3             S           ♣ A K 9 6 5
              ♠ J 9 6 3
              ♡ K Q J 5
              ♦ A 9 2
              ♣ Q 4
```

HAND 42
Dealer West
N–S Vulnerable

                    ♠ Q 6 5 3
                    ♡ 8 7 6 3
                    ◇ A Q 3
                    ♣ 6 4

                        N
                    W   E
                        S

                    ♠ K 10
                    ♡ A 5 4 2
                    ◇ K 7 6
                    ♣ A K 5 3

The Bidding

WEST	NORTH	EAST	SOUTH
No	No	No	1♣
No	1♠	No	1NT
No	2♣	No	2♡
No	4♡	end	

After your precision club, the 1 ♠ reply showed 8–10, balanced, 1NT and a Stayman sequence followed.

West leads the jack of diamonds; plan the play.

With the obvious spade loser, you can see that you are doomed unless the trumps break 3–2. You will need to ruff both your losing clubs in dummy and the danger is that the hand with the doubleton heart also has a doubleton club; now the defence may take three trump tricks. You must therefore draw exactly two rounds of trumps before the ruffing. To avoid a third round, you must duck the first round and put your ace on the second so that you hold the lead. That, however is not the full story. As the ace of spades is with the long trumps, you must keep the king of diamonds in hand as an entry for the second club ruff. Thus the first trick and the diamond return after the heart duck must be won in dummy.

The deal:

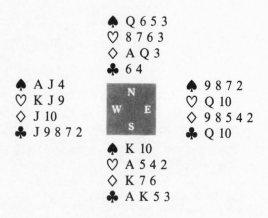

♠ Q 6 5 3
♡ 8 7 6 3
◇ A Q 3
♣ 6 4

♠ A J 4
♡ K J 9
◇ J 10
♣ J 9 8 7 2

♠ 9 8 7 2
♡ Q 10
◇ 9 8 5 4 2
♣ Q 10

♠ K 10
♡ A 5 4 2
◇ K 7 6
♣ A K 5 3

PART 3 DEFENCE BY EAST

HAND 43
Dealer East
Love all

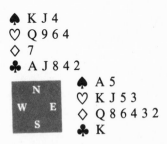

♠ K J 4
♡ Q 9 6 4
◇ 7
♣ A J 8 4 2

♠ A 5
♡ K J 5 3
◇ Q 8 6 4 3 2
♣ K

The Bidding

WEST	NORTH	EAST	SOUTH
		1◇	1♠
No	4♠	end	

Partner leads the seven of spades to dummy's jack and your ace. You continue trumps, South's queen winning. He plays the ten of clubs to partner's seven, dummy's two and your king. How do you continue?

The magic question has to be applied to your partner's opening lead. Despite your bid he has chosen to lead a trump. This can only indicate that he suspects a crossruff. That in turn implies that he has quite a few points and believes that the opponents are very light in this respect. Furthermore, he must believe that the side suits are stopped. It is already bad enough that he has only the queen in clubs (assuming that is the case). The one thing you can be sure of is that he has the ace of hearts otherwise the trump lead has no justification at all. You must therefore switch to a heart before the clubs come in.

The deal:

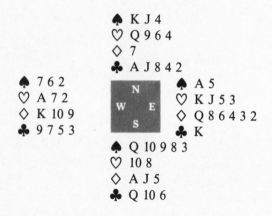

When this deal came up, I was West and with seven points opposite a minimum eleven, it was clear that opponents had bid on distribution. Very often a Precision 1◊ conceals a club holding and I thought it likely that North was short in diamonds and South in clubs. Well, I was half-right. My partner simply didn't ask himself the magic question.

HAND 44
Dealer South
N–S Vulnerable

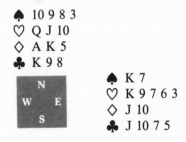

♠ 10 9 8 3
♡ Q J 10
◇ A K 5
♣ K 9 8

♠ K 7
♡ K 9 7 6 3
◇ J 10
♣ J 10 7 5

The Bidding

SOUTH	WEST	NORTH	EAST
1♠	No	2♣	No
3♣	No	4♠	end

South's opener showed 11–15 with 5 plus spades. North now had a very awkward choice, particularly as 1NT would be nonforcing. A direct 4♠ seems most practical but especially at this vulnerability, it could be misinterpreted. North preferred to show a delayed game raise. South's 3♣ bid showed 11–13, probably with 4 plus clubs, but perhaps 5-2-3-3 or 5-3-2-3 with points concentrated in the black suits so that the standard system bid of 2NT was unattractive.

Partner leads the four of diamonds to dummy's king, your jack and South's two. The queen of hearts is now played; plan your defence.

The play to trick one indicates that your partner started with five diamonds and therefore declarer probably has a loser. South does not know that you have four clubs and he does not seem interested in drawing trumps and discarding his losing diamond in dummy on the fourth club if they break. Thus, either he has only three clubs or he thinks it is more likely that he can dispose of his loser on hearts. The key question is who has got the ace of hearts. If partner has it, you must rise with the king now to keep his entry intact otherwise you can't enjoy the diamond winner. If he hasn't, you are going to look very silly if you cover, giving three heart tricks instead of two, which could be fatal. There are two guides which favour covering. Firstly, if South has the ace, partner will have chosen to lead from queen rather than the possibly safer x x x, in hearts. Secondly, in this case you can see that a great deal is lying well for declarer and it may be that all you will be giving away is an overtrick. You should therefore, play your king and continue diamonds.

The deal:

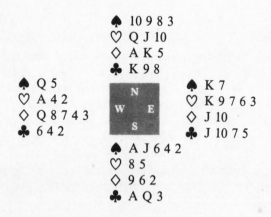

[102]

HAND 45

Dealer West
E–W Vulnerable

```
              ♠ A 6 3 2
              ♡ 8 5 4
              ◇ J 6 2
              ♣ K 6 3
                        ♠ J 8
                        ♡ Q J 10 9 6 3
                        ◇ 9 4
                        ♣ A 8 4
```

The Bidding

WEST	NORTH	EAST	SOUTH
No	No	2♡	2NT
No	3NT	end	

Your opener showed 7–10 with exactly six hearts to at least one of the top three honours. South's 2NT showed about 17–20, balanced.

Partner's lead of the seven of hearts is won by South's ace. He plays the two of clubs to partner's five and dummy's king; plan your defence.

Even giving South a minimum 17, the best you can hope for is seven points with partner and they are unlikely to produce four tricks to add to your ace of clubs. You should thus take the view that you are not going to beat this contract unless your hearts can be brought in. To achieve this, you must hang on to your ace and duck without a flicker hoping that South has the queen and ten of clubs and will be deceived. This hand comes from a major pairs event. I was West and my partner was quick to point out his own error when he won the club leaving declarer with nine tricks.

The deal:

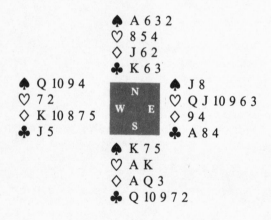

HAND 46

Dealer North
Love all

```
              ♠ 6 5
              ♡ A Q J
              ◇ 7 6 4
              ♣ K 10 4 3 2
```
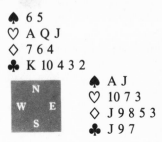
```
                              ♠ A J
                              ♡ 10 7 3
                              ◇ J 9 8 5 3
                              ♣ J 9 7
```

The Bidding

WEST	NORTH	EAST	SOUTH
	No	No	1♠
No	2♣	No	3NT
end			

South is likely to have at least 16.

Partner's opening lead of the two of diamonds is won by South's king. He continues with the two of hearts to partner's five and dummy's queen and follows with the six of spades; plan your defence.

The magic question must be applied to your partner's opening lead. Declarer must have at least two diamonds if his bidding makes sense. If partner has led a singleton in an attempt to find your suit, there is clearly no hope for the defence. You must, therefore, hope that partner led from three to an honour and declarer has the other two honours. Specifically, if partner has A 10 2 and declarer K Q, you may take the first or second round of spades and continue diamonds to defeat the contract. That is provided, of course that you did not play your jack at trick one! When this hand came up, I played 'third man high' without sufficient thought and ruined a brilliant opening lead by partner.

The deal:

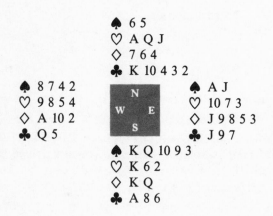

HAND 47
Dealer East
N–S Vulnerable

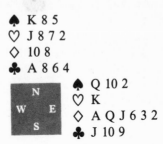

♠ K 8 5
♡ J 8 7 2
♢ 10 8
♣ A 8 6 4

♠ Q 10 2
♡ K
♢ A Q J 6 3 2
♣ J 10 9

The Bidding

WEST	NORTH	EAST	SOUTH
		1♢	1♡
No	3♡	No	4♡
end			

You see that North has a very high opinion of his partner's vulnerable overcalls.

Your partner leads the seven of diamonds; dummy plays the eight. Plan your defence.

It's possible that this lead is a singleton but unlikely, particularly as partner did not double. You should, therefore, turn your attention to the black suits. Your solid club holding makes the suit seem an attractive lead. But it's unlikely that tricks for the defence in that quarter will run away. If, however, South is strong in clubs, tricks in spades could disappear on the long club. You need to find partner with one spade honour. Therefore, take your diamond ace and switch to the two of spades.

The deal:

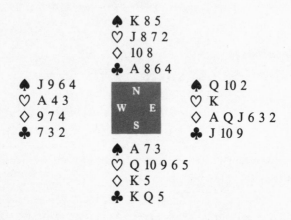

```
              ♠ K 8 5
              ♡ J 8 7 2
              ◇ 10 8
              ♣ A 8 6 4
♠ J 9 6 4                      ♠ Q 10 2
♡ A 4 3        N               ♡ K
◇ 9 7 4      W   E             ◇ A Q J 6 3 2
♣ 7 3 2        S               ♣ J 10 9
              ♠ A 7 3
              ♡ Q 10 9 6 5
              ◇ K 5
              ♣ K Q 5
```

The long club cannot be enjoyed until trumps are drawn and you are just in time.

HAND 48
Dealer South
E–W Vulnerable

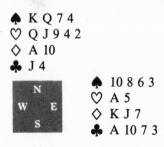

                    ♠ K Q 7 4
                    ♡ Q J 9 4 2
                    ◇ A 10
                    ♣ J 4
                                    ♠ 10 8 6 3
                                    ♡ A 5
                                    ◇ K J 7
                                    ♣ A 10 7 3

The Bidding

    SOUTH   WEST   NORTH   EAST
    2♡   No   4♡   end

The opening bid showed 7–10 with exactly six hearts.

    Partner leads the two of clubs on which dummy plays the
four; plan your defence.

The bidding and lead mark South with king to six hearts and probably three clubs to an honour; partner would hardly have underled king-queen on that auction. With dummy's spade honours well-placed, urgent action is needed to prevent discards. Note declarer need be in no hurry to draw trumps. You can thus see that the three critical cards are the ace of spades, the queen of diamonds and the king of clubs and that partner will need to have two of them if you are to have any chance of success. If you try any of the three possible combinations you will see that winning the ace of clubs and switching to a diamond can only gain and cannot cost. That, therefore, must be your defence. Note that cashing the ace of trumps for a signal fails if South has a singleton ace of spades as you have given him a quick entry to dummy.

The deal:

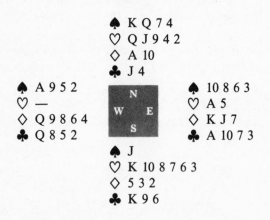

♠ K Q 7 4
♥ Q J 9 4 2
♦ A 10
♣ J 4

♠ A 9 5 2
♥ —
♦ Q 9 8 6 4
♣ Q 8 5 2

♠ 10 8 6 3
♥ A 5
♦ K J 7
♣ A 10 7 3

♠ J
♥ K 10 8 7 6 3
♦ 5 3 2
♣ K 9 6

HAND 49
Dealer West
Game all

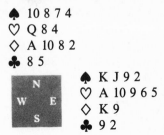

♠ 10 8 7 4
♡ Q 8 4
◇ A 10 8 2
♣ 8 5

♠ K J 9 2
♡ A 10 9 6 5
◇ K 9
♣ 9 2

The Bidding

WEST	NORTH	EAST	SOUTH
No	No	1♡	3NT
end			

South will have, at the very least, a long solid minor and a heart stop.

Partner leads the two of hearts and dummy plays low; plan your defence.

With the king of hearts almost certainly with South, you can see that the ace of diamonds and probably seven club tricks will give the opposition their game; in other words you must take five tricks now or never. A simple process of elimination will pin-point spades as the only hope. West will certainly have to have the ace but the queen may be against you. To cater for Q x with South, you should rise with the ace of hearts and lead the king of spades to ensure four tricks in the suit.

The deal:

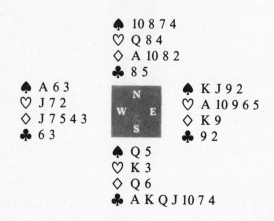

```
              ♠ 10 8 7 4
              ♡ Q 8 4
              ◇ A 10 8 2
              ♣ 8 5
♠ A 6 3                          ♠ K J 9 2
♡ J 7 2            N             ♡ A 10 9 6 5
◇ J 7 5 4 3     W     E          ◇ K 9
♣ 6 3              S             ♣ 9 2
              ♠ Q 5
              ♡ K 3
              ◇ Q 6
              ♣ A K Q J 10 7 4
```

Hopefully, if West has ♠A Q x, he will realise the position and play one of his honours!

HAND 50

Dealer North
N–S Vulnerable

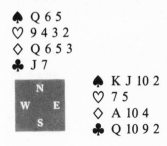

```
          ♠ Q 6 5
          ♡ 9 4 3 2
          ◇ Q 6 5 3
          ♣ J 7
                        ♠ K J 10 2
                        ♡ 7 5
                        ◇ A 10 4
                        ♣ Q 10 9 2
```

The Bidding

WEST	NORTH	EAST	SOUTH
	No	No	1♣
No	1◇	No	2NT
No	3♣	No	3♡
No	4♡	end	

After South's 16 plus opener and North's negative response (less than 8), South's rebid showed 20–21, balanced. A Baron sequence followed.

Partner leads the six of hearts to South's jack. Declarer continues to draw trumps with the ace and king, partner following with the ten and eight. Now comes the king of diamonds on which your partner plays the two and you duck. On South's jack of diamonds partner plays the nine; plan your defence.

It does not matter whether you win the second diamond or keep your ace for the third round. Then you must switch to spades. Partner's carding on both trumps and diamonds indicated an interest in spades and he must surely have the ace. At least two tricks and possibly three are available to you in that suit. Can you see the danger? The standard card from your holding is the jack but if you play it, partner may credit South with something like:

♠Kxxx ♡AKQJ ◇KJx ♣Kx

and duck.

You should therefore, clarify your wishes by playing the two of spades, giving partner no reason to duck. You should also have discarded one of the minor tens on the third round of trumps to express an interest in spades.

The deal:

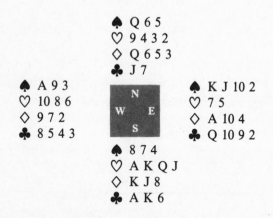

```
                    ♠ Q 6 5
                    ♡ 9 4 3 2
                    ◇ Q 6 5 3
                    ♣ J 7
   ♠ A 9 3            N          ♠ K J 10 2
   ♡ 10 8 6        W     E       ♡ 7 5
   ◇ 9 7 2            S          ◇ A 10 4
   ♣ 8 5 4 3                     ♣ Q 10 9 2
                    ♠ 8 7 4
                    ♡ A K Q J
                    ◇ K J 8
                    ♣ A K 6
```

HAND 51

Dealer South
Game all

    ♠ K Q 7 6
    ♡ 10 5
    ◇ 10 7 6
    ♣ A Q 6 3

                    ♠ 10 8 3
                    ♡ 8 7 4
                    ◇ A K J 9 8
                    ♣ K 5

The Bidding

SOUTH	WEST	NORTH	EAST
1NT	No	2♣	No
2◇	No	2NT	No
3NT	end		

The 12–14 opener was followed by Stayman.

Partner's lead of the queen of hearts is won by South's ace. He follows with the jack of clubs to partner's two and dummy's three; plan your defence.

Partner's lead marks him with three points in hearts and with the other three jacks now visible, you can effectively see all points available to the defence. Now, if you complete the roll call by counting the suits, you should realise that partner's club marks South with four and he has failed to find a four-card major. He must, therefore have at least three diamonds to the queen. To set the contract, you must bring in your diamond suit and you have worked out that banging down ace and king is hopeless. The best chance is to lead the jack first time. South may cover and take ten tricks but he is more likely to play you for KJ9xx or AJ9xx, in which case he must play low or go two off. This defence is particularly likely to succeed as you will have already produced the king of clubs and have not bid. You should thus win the club and switch to the jack of diamonds. You may get away with ducking the first club but there is no reason to do so and worse still, partner is likely to play the eight of clubs on the second round to encourage hearts and South may smell a rat.

The deal:

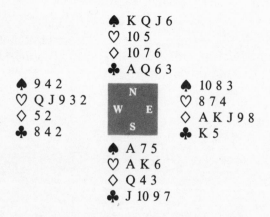

HAND 52
Dealer West
Love all

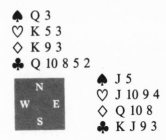

```
            ♠ Q 3
            ♡ K 5 3
            ◇ K 9 3
            ♣ Q 10 8 5 2
                        ♠ J 5
                        ♡ J 10 9 4
                        ◇ Q 10 8
                        ♣ K J 9 3
```

The Bidding

WEST	NORTH	EAST	SOUTH
No	No	No	1 ◇
No	2 ♣	No	3NT
end			

Your partner's lead of the six of spades is won by dummy's queen. Declarer calls for the king of diamonds from dummy, clearly intending to continue the suit as his principal source of tricks. Plan your defence.

Again a count of points and suits will guide you to your only hope of defeating the contract. South's bidding marks him with at least 16 and with 19 more in view, the best partner can have is 5. The clubs are well placed for you but you can see that partner will not have nearly enough entries to bring them in. Your only hope, therefore, lies in spades. South's failure to bid them and partner's lead suggests that he might have A 10 x x x x. In that case you have five tricks in the suit provided two conditions are fulfilled. Firstly, you must avoid blocking the suit by throwing the jack under the queen on trick one. Secondly, you must hope that you can get the lead in time. For that, partner will need to have the jack of diamonds. You must play your eight on the king and rise with the queen on the next round swallowing the jack in what is known as the crocodile coup. Now declarer cannot lose a diamond to the safe West hand and must be held to seven tricks.

The deal:

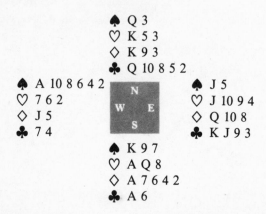

♠ Q 3
♡ K 5 3
♢ K 9 3
♣ Q 10 8 5 2

♠ A 10 8 6 4 2
♡ 7 6 2
♢ J 5
♣ 7 4

♠ J 5
♡ J 10 9 4
♢ Q 10 8
♣ K J 9 3

♠ K 9 7
♡ A Q 8
♢ A 7 6 4 2
♣ A 6

As the cards lie, of course, the game can be made if declarer ducks the first round of spades completely in both hands. However, this is unlikely in practice as this line of play gives up the chance of a second stop which will be needed if the suit breaks 5–3.

HAND 53
Dealer North
E–W Vulnerable

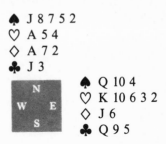

```
          ♠ J 8 7 5 2
          ♡ A 5 4
          ◇ A 7 2
          ♣ J 3
                      ♠ Q 10 4
              N       ♡ K 10 6 3 2
          W       E   ◇ J 6
              S       ♣ Q 9 5
```

The Bidding

WEST	NORTH	EAST	SOUTH
	No	No	1♠
No	3♠	No	4♣
No	4◇	No	5♣
No	5♡	No	7♠
end			

After spades had been agreed, all subsequent bids were cue bids.

On your partner's lead of the queen of hearts, dummy's ace is played; plan your defence.

As far as trick one is concerned, I am not too worried which card you play; but it pays not to be spectacular. A quietly encouraging six is probably best. What is vital is to realise that South is likely to have the five outstanding spades, in which case it will cost him nothing to lead the jack from dummy in case you cover or hesitate. You should be prepared to duck nonchalantly.

The deal:

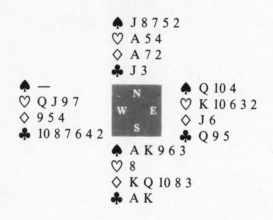

```
              ♠ J 8 7 5 2
              ♡ A 5 4
              ◇ A 7 2
              ♣ J 3
♠ —                           ♠ Q 10 4
♡ Q J 9 7        N            ♡ K 10 6 3 2
◇ 9 5 4      W       E        ◇ J 6
♣ 10 8 7 6 4 2      S         ♣ Q 9 5
              ♠ A K 9 6 3
              ♡ 8
              ◇ K Q 10 8 3
              ♣ A K
```

HAND 54
Dealer East
Game all

```
                   ♠ 4
                   ♡ K Q 5
                   ◇ Q 9
                   ♣ A J 10 9 8 5 3
                              ♠ 10 9 7 5 3 2
                        N     ♡ 9 7 6 4
                     W     E  ◇ K 5 2
                        S     ♣ —
```

The Bidding

WEST	NORTH	EAST	SOUTH
		No	1♣
No	2♣	No	2NT
No	3♣	No	4♣
No	4NT	No	5♠
No	7♣	end	

After the 16 plus opening, the 2♣ bid showed 8 plus with at least five clubs. 2NT was an enquiry for more information and 3♣ confirmed a six-card or longer suit implying no other biddable suit. 4♣ from South asked his partner to start cue-bidding side aces. 4NT said that North had no first-round control but was nevertheless interested in a slam; thus the inference was that he had the ace of trumps and more points and/or clubs than originally promised. 5♠ showed all the other controls and an interest in a possible grand slam. North took the view that the grand would, at the worst, be on a finesse and could well be cold.

Partner leads the jack of hearts to dummy's king, your six and South's three. The four of spades is led from dummy to your five, South's ace and partner's six. South continues with the eight of spades, ruffing your partner's jack and now leads the three of trumps; plan your defence.

[121]

Partner has already shown up with two jacks and in order to justify his bidding, South ought to have at least 20 points and probably more. The very best you can hope for is another queen in the West hand. Both red queens are visible and if partner has the queen of spades, you can see that the diamond loser can be discarded on the second top spade leaving no problem. Now let's ask the magic question regarding the play so far. Why did South win the first trick in dummy specifically and what was the hurry to play spades like that? All this completes the picture. Partner has the queen of clubs and declarer is trying to shorten his trumps in preparation for a 4–0 split. That is why he had to keep the ace of hearts intact; he needs every entry he can get to be able to ruff spades. That is where you come in. South needs five entries to his hand. Three to ruff spades, one to take the first club finesse and one at trick eleven to be able to lead a diamond at trick twelve for the ruffing finesse. Three aces and the king of clubs cannot be touched. The fifth must come from a diamond finesse. You must be ready to put the spoke in the wheel. After the king of clubs, South will take the marked trump finesse, cash the queen of hearts, cross to the ace, ruff a spade and play a diamond. If he plays the queen, you must not cover; if he plays the nine, you must put in the king to block the suit.

The deal:

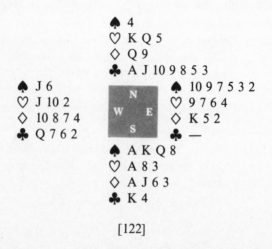

```
              ♠ 4
              ♡ K Q 5
              ◇ Q 9
              ♣ A J 10 9 8 5 3
♠ J 6                        ♠ 10 9 7 5 3 2
♡ J 10 2          N          ♡ 9 7 6 4
◇ 10 8 7 4     W     E       ◇ K 5 2
♣ Q 7 6 2         S          ♣ —
              ♠ A K Q 8
              ♡ A 8 3
              ◇ A J 6 3
              ♣ K 4
```

HAND 55

Dealer South
Love all

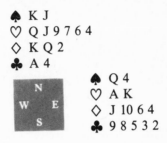

♠ K J
♡ Q J 9 7 6 4
◇ K Q 2
♣ A 4

♠ Q 4
♡ A K
◇ J 10 6 4
♣ 9 8 5 3 2

The Bidding

SOUTH	WEST	NORTH	EAST
No	No	1♡	No
1♠	No	3♡	No
3NT	end		

Partner leads the nine of diamonds to the two, six and ace. South plays the ten of hearts and West follows with the eight, dummy plays low and you win. How do you continue?

The bidding and play so far clarifies that there is no future in diamonds and that you can't afford to play passive with a long heart suit coming in shortly. The magic question should be directed to that eight of hearts. Surely with a large number of entries to dummy, the count is of little relevance and even if you are a compulsive numerologist, how many hearts has West got? If it's two, then why didn't South support hearts? If it's four, then West has ♡ 8 5 3 2 and the five would have been sufficient. No, this must be a desperate suit indication from a partner who is praying for you to have the queen of spades. You should clarify the position by leading it now.

The deal:

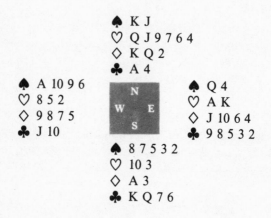

```
                        ♠ K J
                        ♡ Q J 9 7 6 4
                        ◇ K Q 2
                        ♣ A 4
  ♠ A 10 9 6                         ♠ Q 4
  ♡ 8 5 2            N               ♡ A K
  ◇ 9 8 7 5     W         E          ◇ J 10 6 4
  ♣ J 10             S               ♣ 9 8 5 3 2
                        ♠ 8 7 5 3 2
                        ♡ 10 3
                        ◇ A 3
                        ♣ K Q 7 6
```

Actually, the four of spades is good enough as West can duck completely, but the queen is much easier to read.

HAND 56
Dealer West
N–S Vulnerable

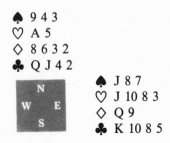

♠ 9 4 3
♡ A 5
◇ 8 6 3 2
♣ Q J 4 2

♠ J 8 7
♡ J 10 8 3
◇ Q 9
♣ K 10 8 5

The Bidding

WEST	NORTH	EAST	SOUTH
No	No	No	2NT
No	3NT	end	

The opener showed 20–22.

Partner's lead of the two of hearts goes to dummy's five, your ten and South's king. Declarer now leads the six of clubs to partner's three and dummy's jack; plan your defence.

South probably has three or four clubs to the ace and I think it will pay to duck smoothly in this situation. Satisfied that the king is with West, declarer will almost certainly play back to his ace and if West can follow, you will get two tricks if a third round is played. Note two points: South cannot 'keep control' by playing the second round from his hand; the entry position does not permit it. West could win and knock out the ace of hearts. Also your partner did well not to give a count. If you win the first club, South can test spades in time as he has only lost one club trick. To be able to work this out in good time, it has become accepted procedure for the player sitting over dummy to be allowed time to work out his defence of the whole hand at trick one. If you have nothing to think about on that trick one, place your ten of hearts on the table face down so that declarer is not fooled by a false hesitation.

The deal:

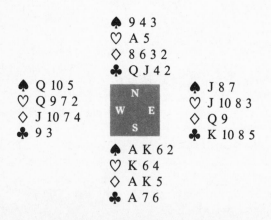

```
            ♠ 9 4 3
            ♡ A 5
            ◇ 8 6 3 2
            ♣ Q J 4 2
♠ Q 10 5                      ♠ J 8 7
♡ Q 9 7 2        N            ♡ J 10 8 3
◇ J 10 7 4    W     E         ◇ Q 9
♣ 9 3            S            ♣ K 10 8 5
            ♠ A K 6 2
            ♡ K 6 4
            ◇ A K 5
            ♣ A 7 6
```

If declarer falls for your ruse, he must lose five tricks. So, if you fully realised the point of the problem, not later than at the end of trick one, and were ready to duck without thought, you may assume that you defeated the contract.

HAND 57
Dealer North
Game all

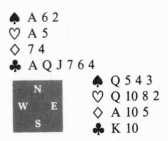

```
          ♠ A 6 2
          ♡ A 5
          ◇ 7 4
          ♣ A Q J 7 6 4
                         ♠ Q 5 4 3
             N           ♡ Q 10 8 2
          W     E        ◇ A 10 5
             S           ♣ K 10
```

The Bidding

WEST	NORTH	EAST	SOUTH
	1♣	No	1♡
No	3♣	No	3◇
No	3♠	No	3NT
end			

North's 3♠ bid was directional asking, hoping for at least a half-stop in spades.

Partner leads the ten of spades to the two, queen and king. Now the nine of clubs is played to the two and jack; plan your defence.

The play to trick one indicates that South has three spade tricks and with the clubs coming in, there are plenty of tricks in total for the contract. You must, therefore, take five tricks now or never. There is nothing to be gained by ducking the club and indeed it could present declarer with the contract. As you will see below, he may well play the ace next as his principal concern is to keep you, rather than West, off play. Obviously, your only hope for a quick break-through lies in diamonds which implies that partner will have to hold at least the king and jack with two others. The critical case arises when he has KJ8x when two leads will be required from your side without blocking the suit. On winning the club, you must switch to the ten of diamonds.

The deal:

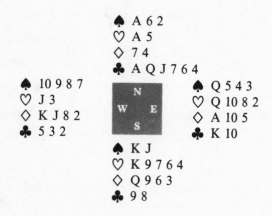

```
                 ♠ A 6 2
                 ♡ A 5
                 ◇ 7 4
                 ♣ A Q J 7 6 4
  ♠ 10 9 8 7                      ♠ Q 5 4 3
  ♡ J 3           N              ♡ Q 10 8 2
  ◇ K J 8 2    W     E           ◇ A 10 5
  ♣ 5 3 2          S             ♣ K 10
                 ♠ K J
                 ♡ K 9 7 6 4
                 ◇ Q 9 6 3
                 ♣ 9 8
```

Arguably, South should have rejected the club finesse altogether and protected against a singleton king in your hand. However, there was the more likely possibility of West having ♣ K 10 x x in which case two finesses are needed to prevent two club losers.

HAND 58
Dealer East
Love all

♠ 10
♡ A Q 10 8 6
◇ K 10 8 2
♣ J 9 8

♠ A 7 3
♡ 9 5 2
◇ 9 6
♣ Q 10 7 5 3

The Bidding

WEST	NORTH	EAST	SOUTH
		No	1◇
No	1♡	No	3◇
No	5◇	end	

Partner leads the ace of clubs. You play an encouraging seven whereupon he cashes the king of clubs, all following, and switches to the five of spades to dummy's ten; plan your defence.

This could hardly be simpler. You just take the ace of spades, concede the rest of the tricks to declarer and go on to the next deal. But . . . which club did you play at trick two? When this hand came up, I played low whereupon partner played a third club and my spade trick vanished.

The deal:

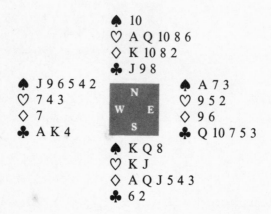

Partner cannot see your ace of spades and has little reason to ignore your club encouragement unless you cancel it by playing the ten or queen second time. It could be argued that you should discourage clubs on the first round as the second club trick can be taken after the spade has been cashed. However, this could set partner on to the wrong track. Particularly if he is weak in hearts, he might think you have that suit heavily stacked over dummy and might therefore think it correct to switch to trumps, with disastrous results. A case can be made for playing the queen of clubs at trick one.

HAND 59
Dealer South
N–S Vulnerable

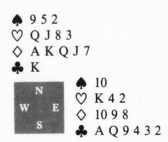

```
        ♠ 9 5 2
        ♡ Q J 8 3
        ◇ A K Q J 7
        ♣ K
                        ♠ 10
                        ♡ K 4 2
                        ◇ 10 9 8
                        ♣ A Q 9 4 3 2
```

The Bidding

SOUTH	WEST	NORTH	EAST
No	2♠	Double	No
3NT	end		

Partner's opener showed 7–10 with exactly six spades. The double was for take-out.

Partner leads the eight of clubs. You win and return the ten of spades to the ace, six and two. Now comes the five of hearts to the six and jack; plan your defence.

The opening lead marks South with ♣J10xx and your partner's failure to lead a spade indicates a weak suit so South is likely to have two stops (as his bidding more or less confirms). If he has anything in hearts, the defence has no hope and you will have to credit partner with at least A10x. South has seven top tricks in spades and diamonds and you must ensure that he does not develop two more before partner's spades are established. There are two possible lines of defence. You can win this heart trick and return the ten of diamonds. Declarer can now take eight tricks by running all the diamonds, discarding a spade and a club from hand. West must hold on to the ten of hearts otherwise the suit can be set up. If he discards the eight of clubs, declarer returns to hand with the spade king and leads towards dummy's hearts ensuring eight tricks that way. If West holds on to both cards, he will have to discard three spades and the defence can now take five tricks only.

Alternatively, you may duck the heart and arrange not to take a heart trick in your hand at all, allowing partner to get in twice to set up and enjoy his spades. Thus you will cover the queen of hearts or duck the three.

The deal:

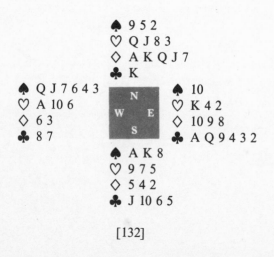

HAND 60

Dealer West
E–W Vulnerable

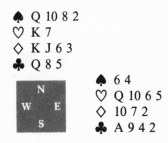

♠ Q 10 8 2
♡ K 7
◇ K J 6 3
♣ Q 8 5

♠ 6 4
♡ Q 10 6 5
◇ 10 7 2
♣ A 9 4 2

The Bidding

WEST	NORTH	EAST	SOUTH
No	No	No	1NT
No	2♣	No	2♠
No	3♠	No	4♠
end			

A 12–14 1NT was followed by a Stayman sequence.

On your partner's opening lead of the eight of diamonds dummy plays low and declarer's ace wins. He leads a low spade to your partner's king and West returns the five of diamonds to South's queen. Another low spade goes to partner's ace and he now leads the seven of clubs to dummy's eight; plan your defence.

A very easy hand to finish with. You know that partner started with a doubleton diamond so you simply go up with the ace of clubs to give him his ruff. On the bidding, South can only have four trumps so partner is bound to have one more. Is this familiar? You're right – it's Hand 1 all over again except that while you walked round the table, I switched the suits round.

The deal:

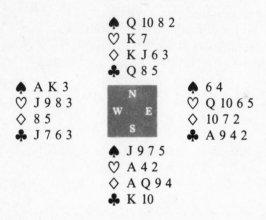

```
                    ♠ Q 10 8 2
                    ♡ K 7
                    ◇ K J 6 3
                    ♣ Q 8 5
  ♠ A K 3              N              ♠ 6 4
  ♡ J 9 8 3       W       E          ♡ Q 10 6 5
  ◇ 8 5               S              ◇ 10 7 2
  ♣ J 7 6 3                          ♣ A 9 4 2
                    ♠ J 9 7 5
                    ♡ A 4 2
                    ◇ A Q 9 4
                    ♣ K 10
```

Oh! By the way . . . you did, of course, play the two of diamonds at trick one to clarify to your partner which of clubs and hearts was needed as a switch to get you on lead. You didn't? Then I am afraid he got it wrong and declarer made the contract. Furthermore, if you missed this point on hand 1, you have effectively made the same mistake twice. Promise that you will never let that happen again.

THE POST-MORTEM

Well, how did you get on? The most important thing is that you enjoyed the quiz and I sincerely hope you did. If, in an atmosphere of intense boredom, you answered all the questions correctly, please accept my apologies for wasting your time and money but even then you may have treasured a welcome boost to your ego. If you suffered a few mishaps, may I invite you to a short investigation to see what, if anything, might be learnt from the set of problems.

Hands 1 and 60	showed the need to give a suit-preference signal on trick 1.
Hands 4 and 28	showed the need to hold the lead to exercise possible options in subsequent play; note this can apply to declarer or defender.
Hands 5, 17, 18, 52	showed the need to unblock a doubleton honour to avoid a blockage in the suit or to avoid being endplayed. Hand 8 however, spelt a word of warning not to do it every time. Nevertheless, when you are defending, a doubleton honour should flash a warning light. Note that illustrations were given involving all four top honours.
Hands 11 and 55	showed the need for the defenders to suspect that a very weak suit has been bid by declarer and that it should be attacked despite a strong holding in dummy.

[135]

Hands 20 and 23	indicated that you can enjoy a ruff even if there is a trebleton in dummy. I should hesitate, however, to count on that in the bidding!
Hands 21, 27, 41	demonstrated that there are often small but cheap extra chances of capturing a bare or poorly protected king. It is worth remembering that when you are missing a king, there are alternatives to finessing . . . which will work only half the time anyway!
Hands 26 and 39	emphasised the importance of clearing a side suit to cut the enemy communications. Note that in one case the idea was to avoid a ruff, while in the other the aim was to stop them playing trumps to prevent your ruffing.

Finally, on several occasions, the clue to success was through asking yourself the magic question following a strange play or, as in hand 3, apparently inconsistent bidding. It assisted card-reading almost beyond measure and for me, that is the principal message of this book. Hopefully, you are now a better player!